Family Therapy

Family Therapy
Combining Psychodynamic
and Family Systems Approaches

Edited by

John K. Pearce, M.D.
Cambridge Family Institute
Cambridge, Massachusetts

Leonard J. Friedman, M.D.
Harvard Medical School and
Cambridge Family Institute
Cambridge, Massachusetts

GRUNE & STRATTON
A Subsidiary of Harcourt Brace Jovanovich, Publishers
NEW YORK   LONDON   TORONTO   SYDNEY   SAN FRANCISCO

Library of Congress Cataloging in Publication Data
Main entry under title:
Family therapy.

Bibliography: p.
Includes index.
1.   Family psychotherapy.   I.   Pearce, John K.,
1935–   II.   Friedman, Leonard J.   [DNLM: 1.   Family
therapy.   WM430.5.F2 F199]
RC488.5.F323   616.89′156   79-27047
ISBN 0-8089-1245-3

Grune & Stratton, Inc.
111 Fifth Avenue
New York, New York 10003

Distributed in the United Kingdom by
Academic Press, Inc. (London) Ltd.
24/28 Oval Road, London NW 1

Library of Congress Catalog Number 79-27047
International Standard Book Number 0-8089-1245-3
Printed in the United States of America

Contents

Foreword

Back in the early 1960s, when we were flush with excitement about what we were learning by seeing whole families, I gave some talks about our findings to various professional groups. I spoke to a psychoanalytic group about something called "family therapy," and I recall that one analyst stood up after my talk and said loudly, "Doctor, you are doing a very dangerous thing, treating parents and children together." Another analyst, world famous, discussed my paper by telling some family jokes. In later years, when the psychoanalytic world began to take family therapy more seriously, the systems perspective was viewed as either unnecessary or was disputed by psychoanalytic logic: "The transference/countertransference would be hopelessly confounded by the family treatment situation." "I do not need to see the family to know what's going on with them; the family is represented in the one mind I am treating." "The environment or families do not make people sick; people do it to themselves via fantasy or intrapsychic elaboration of what goes on outside." "Besides, when the ego gets stronger it will be able to deal with the family pathology." Attempts to incorporate system theory with psychoanalytic concepts were initially strained and awkward, not only because the links between the two different order of phenomena had not yet been found, but also because it was the rare psychoanalyst who directly observed marital or family interaction, much less treated couples or families conjointly. Many psychoanalysts today still are oblivious of family transactional theory, and functionally operate as if the patient lives in a vacuum, as if life stops during analysis. Other psychodynamically oriented therapists, recognizing family theory and therapy as a force to be reckoned with, tried to hop on the bandwagon; some missed the whole point by inviting the family in to get more information about the patient.

The fact that there can be a book like this is evidence of how much has changed since the early days of family therapy. In this volume we have one of the first serious attempts to integrate psychodynamic and system concepts. Represented here are a group of experienced theoretician-therapists, some of them psychoanalysts, all of them trained to deal with the intrapsychic world, and all of them family therapists as well. They share my belief that it is not a question of whether the intrapsychic or transactional is more important, or whether one can be reduced to the other, but that it is the *relationship* between the two that needs to be explored. For me, the interpersonal resolution of inner conflict is what is at the basis of marital and family dysfunction. The creative leap of family-system theory was discovery of the interlocking, multiperson motivational system whereby intimates collusively carry psychic functions for each other— however, those of us who try to integrate what is known about intrapsychic psychology with what goes on between people, especially intimates, have become a minority in the family field. One path taken by some family therapists has been to renounce psychodynamic formulations altogether and focus on interactional patterns and restructuring of relational sequences in the present; the past and what goes on inside peoples' heads is considered irrelevant. (At least this stance is taken in the publications of members of this family therapy school; it is obvious to anyone who observes treatment sessions conducted by these family therapists that they are making constant but implicit use of their psychodynamic knowledge).

The authors of these papers not only present their conceptual outlooks in attempting to bridge psychoanalytic and system concepts, but each one spells out in detail the treatment strategies based upon his or her theory. I have discovered in these papers new ways of looking at clinical problems and creative techniques to try out.

Moss, who makes an interesting distinction between family therapy and family counseling, describes the characteristics and treatment of families containing a severely disturbed member. Earlier in this Foreword I observed that some therapists misinterpret the systems viewpoint by having the family come in to give information about the patient. Moss, who knows system theory, and knows how easily threatened such families are, utilizes this procedure as a strategy for involving the family in treatment.

Chasin and Grunebaum have made one of the few attempts at organizing the various family theories into meaningful categories. They suggest that the sundry family theories and treatment approaches have similarities as well as differences, and that they can enrich each other. A key, intriguing sentence in their paper: "We may wonder what kind of transgenerational history leads to the families with anorexia that have been so carefully described from the interactional perspective."

Eisendrath graphically describes the kinds of family environments that produce borderline patients. Utilizing an object relations approach, he depicts, similar to Laing, how such patients have been systematically inauthenticated and made to distrust their own senses. His treatment strategy consists of "stripping away the family myths."

Strasburger describes a case that started as individual therapy for the wife and later included the husband. He seems to have overcome the risks of converting individual therapy to couple therapy (e.g., the spouse coming in later can enter as a guest to an established relationship between the partner and the therapist). Some new and useful marital therapy techniques are described in this paper.

Friedman, another synthesizer of psychoanalysis (object relations theory in particular) and family-system theory, sees the two conceptual frameworks as complementary. In his chapter, further, there is a refreshingly honest step-by-step account of how he conducts marital therapy, from the first phone contact to the later stages of treatment. I was particularly fascinated by his techniques of having partners imagine what a marriage would have been like between his mother and her father, and her mother and his father. His hypothesis, that when such an imagined marriage is described as disastrous the prognosis for the couple is poor, should be tested.

La Perriere, in a simply written and interesting paper, addresses an area frequently overlooked by family therapists, that of crossing the boundary between the world of the adult and the world of the child. Many family therapists, myself included, have had limited experience treating small children and being able to view the world through the eyes of a small child. Most adults have forgotten what it was like being a child, only sometimes getting in touch with that experience when becoming a parent. There is also an excellent discussion in this paper of the split in our society between adults' professional work world and their personal family life.

Slipp uses his concept of the Symbiotic Survival Pattern as a bridge between the intrapsychic and system perspectives. Like myself, Slipp strongly urges that the field begin to examine how the various family theories can be integrated. We perhaps both do not recognize that some family therapists believe that the search for commonalities is fruitless; there are those who claim that family therapy is a discontinuous step from the past and that there must be a clean break with traditional intrapsychic concepts.

Kantor, in a closely reasoned and solid chapter, gives his explanation for the central problem in marital difficulties: the partners' competing claims about reality. He uses the concept of the critical identity image—the way each person organizes the outside world—to elucidate this universal dilemma in marital and family relationships. One of the other important contributions of this paper is Kantor's effort to develop a common vocabulary for describing families. There is great need in the family field for a widely accepted classification or diagnostic system for families. Kantor's attempt to set up a typology of families that fits the wide variety of family forms and styles should be followed up systematically.

My good friend, John Pearce, is the only family therapist I know who has explored the most neglected area in family therapy training, that of ethnic variations in families. Every family therapist assumes his or her theory and body of techniques is sufficient to treat all ethnic varieties. A Jewish family therapist from the Bronx, however, will have difficulty treating a Norwegian-American farmer family in Minnesota; a WASP family therapist will be confused by the workings of an Irish-American family; and middle class family therapists are often bewildered by poor families of all races. Note that I am not discussing the treatment of families or couples in Europe, Asia, or Africa, who are usually interviewed via an interpreter—another source of dissonance. Although there are universals that cut across all families everywhere, unless one is familiar with a particular ethnic group (its values, ways of thinking and communicating, etc.), one can not only misunderstand, but may misinterpret as pathology, behavior that is normal for that culture (e.g., when immigrant parents from Southern Italy speak of some people having *mal occhio,* the "evil eye").

Like most people who are asked to write a foreword, I am extremely busy and had decided beforehand that I would just skim these papers; instead I got caught up in each one and read them through because they were so stimulating. It is time for synthesis of different viewpoints in the field of family therapy, and this volume is an important step in that direction.

James L. Framo, Ph.D.

Philadelphia, Pennsylvania

Preface

When future historians of psychotherapy look back on the 1960s, it will seem obvious that after the spectacular growth and development of psychoanalytically inspired intrapsychic theory in the previous 50 years, the next step would be to similarly study families. Pioneers in family therapy hoped that the reasonableness and obvious relevance of the family approach would lead to rapid integration with intrapsychic theory. That is not what happened. What happened was more in line with the process described by Thomas S. Kuhn in *The Structure of Scientific Revolutions:* the new ideas threatened established people and were taken up by the adventurous and the young. Now we have reached a middle point, where beginning therapists take it for granted that they should learn about families and senior therapists recognize that there is something to it, even if they are not quite sure what.

The core image for psychoanalysis has been the *individual* as a layered set of structures, with *character* formed by the conflict of stage-specific drive aims with social reality as elaborated in fantasy. Processes are explained in terms of linear causality. Symptoms are seen as *meaningful personal expressions*. The shift of viewpoint engendered by family therapy is to the interactive *context* of development, to circular causality, to *patterns of action*. We believe that both approaches are useful and can be integrated in practice.

This book is the product of an ongoing process. For 8 years, a group of 12 to 20 Cambridge psychotherapists (including 6 of the 9 authors of this book) have met monthly in a literature seminar focused by the reading of a book on family therapy. All are seasoned clinicians trained in the traditions of psychoanalytic psychotherapy. In an eclectic spirit we have read and digested some 80 books and repeatedly gone through cycles of discovery, exhilaration, application to treatment, sharing of results, and gradual consensus about the appropriate application of treatment theories. We almost always had someone in the seminar with firsthand experience with the author of the books chosen for discussion, so we were able to frame the new ideas within the context in which they had appeared, as well as to try out their application within our own worlds.

The seminar members and the contributors to this volume can be characterized in general as skeptical synthesizers with a fondness for new ideas. Over the years we have read and been influenced by works of Bowen, Minuchin, Haley, Ackerman, Berne (whose transactional analysis, though not a family therapy, focuses on sequences of interaction), Spark and Boszormenyi-Nagy, Bateson, Watzlawick, Toman (who is a pioneer in thinking about the consequences of sibling constellations), Henry, Kantor, Erickson (the father of strategic family therapy), Levenson, Satir, psychodramatists, students of ethnicity, and many others. Throughout we have worked toward the integration of these theories.

When Friedman organized the Society for Family Therapy and Research Conference, held in October 1978, that provided the raw material for this book, he included three pioneers in the integration of these two perspectives who were not part of our Cambridge group: Framo, La Perriere, and Slipp. We could not include Framo's stimulating paper in this volume because of a commitment to publish elsewhere, and are delighted that he agreed to be represented by writing the foreword.

A word about the eclectic spirit: there is a traditional quarrel between the seeker of the true, whole, and single truth, and the seeker of the limited, partial truth—the hedgehog and the fox. When it comes to the making of books, the hedgehog has advantages: he has one idea, a good one, and follows it to the limit— even past the limit. It is the hedgehog's nature not really to be very interested in limits, even to fail to mention awkward negative outcomes—a crime in normal science but quite routine in anecdotal psychotherapy literature, where a case, suitably disguised, is intended to exemplify a method or process, and the follow-up on the actual case is seen as irrelevant. Foxes are not more virtuous, but they are interested in the limitations, the failures that occur when ideas are applied in the wrong contexts. They are apt to take an ironic stance toward their partial truths. Our group is rich in such skepticism.

New ideas are always generated by novel perspectives on familiar phenomena or, more often, by looking at new phenomena. The family, as a new phenomenon for direct study, has inspired a variety of new ideas: enmeshment, triangulation, fusion, sequence, and context, to mention a few. The action orientation needed in family work has generated a new set of action techniques. We offer a blending of these and psychodynamic approaches, both practical clinical detail and theoretical elaboration. We hope that readers will be stimulated to try out, expand, elaborate, and innovate from some of these ideas.

John K. Pearce, M.D.
Leonard J. Friedman, M.D.

Cambridge, Massachusetts

Contributors

RICHARD CHASIN, M.D. Assistant Clinical Professor of Psychiatry, Harvard Medical School; Assistant Clinical Professor of Child Psychiatry, Boston University School of Medicine; Faculty, Cambridge Family Institute, Cambridge, Massachusetts.

ROBERT M. EISENDRATH, M.D. Director, Adult Clinic, South Shore Mental Health Center, Quincy, Massachusetts; Assistant Clinical Professor of Psychiatry, Harvard Medical School; Instructor of Clinical Psychiatry, Tufts University School of Medicine, Boston, Massachusetts.

LEONARD J. FRIEDMAN, M.D. Assistant Clinical Professor of Psychiatry, Harvard Medical School; Faculty, Cambridge Family Institute, Cambridge, Massachusetts.

HENRY GRUNEBAUM, M.D. Director, Group and Family Psychotherapy Training, Cambridge Hospital; Associate Clinical Professor of Psychiatry, Harvard Medical School, Boston, Massachusetts.

DAVID KANTOR, Ph.D. Director, Cambridge Family Institute; Faculty, Tufts University School of Medicine, Boston, Massachusetts.

KITTY LA PERRIERE, Ph.D. Director of Education, Ackerman Institute for Family Therapy, New York, New York.

NORMAN I. MOSS, M.D.   Associate in Psychiatry, Beth Israel Hospital, Boston; Clinical Instructor in Psychiatry, Harvard Medical School, Boston, Massachusetts.

JOHN K. PEARCE, M.D.   Faculty, Cambridge Family Institute, Cambridge, Massachusetts.

SAMUEL SLIPP, M.D.   Clinical Professor of Psychiatry, New York University School of Medicine, New York, New York.

LARRY H. STRASBURGER, M.D.   Clinical Instructor in Psychiatry, Harvard Medical School, Boston, Massachusetts.

Richard Chasin, M.D.
Henry Grunebaum, M.D.

1

A Brief Synopsis of Current Concepts and Practices in Family Therapy

Family therapy is not a unified theory about families. It is not group therapy in which the group members happen to be related to each other. Rather, it is a vast array of techniques, all guided by a cluster of major concepts about family systems. We would like to present a scheme to help classify, organize and explicate that aggregate of theories and techniques which comprise family therapy today.

Our scheme organizes the principal concepts and practices of family therapy into three basic diagnostic perspectives and three basic treatment approaches. Such a scheme can be applied to individual or group therapy. In this synopsis it will be applied to family therapy. In order to remain brief, many important theories and theorists will have to be omitted from this paper. Furthermore, this presentation might make each theorist who is represented seem as though he or she has contributed to only one perspective or to one approach. Far from it, the best of them have contributed to all the perspectives and all the approaches.

DIAGNOSTIC PERSPECTIVES

There are three types of diagnostic theories: (1) those that explain the family predicament from an *historic* perspective; (2) those that describe family behavior from an *interactional* perspec-

1

tive; (3) those that depict the quality of family life from an *experiential* perspective.

To clarify these perspectives, we might use the analogy of an automobile mechanic. Looking at a car from an historic perspective, he might ask, "What on earth happened to this thing?" Approaching the car from an interactional perspective, he might search the engine for faulty interplay among its parts. Finally, he may employ an experiential perspective by road-testing the car to get a "feel" for its problem. This mechanic may learn something different about the car from each of these perspectives.

We would like to describe a few concepts that bear on each perspective. For clinical illustration, we shall use a single fictitious family: John and Mary, father and mother of Peggy, a teenager.

The Historic Perspective

UNRESOLVED ISSUES

Paul and Paul (1975) theorize that unresolved issues in one generation inevitably distress subsequent generations. They indicate that an unresolved loss may not only affect the bereaved— in the way Freud describes in *Mourning and Melancholia*—but it may affect the progeny as well.

John lost his mother when he was a young boy, but he had no grief reaction. He had been intensely ambivalent about her. Emblems of that ambivalence were the ways he cringed at her whining complaints and the delight he took in her unexpected smiling glances. Years later, whenever his daughter Peggy whined, John left the room. Peggy became an uncomplaining girl who rarely was aware of being displeased even in situations that might have infuritated others. In fact, she softened moments of great stress with her ever-smiling eyes. Once John referred to her eyes as the "light of his life." Most of Peggy's friends left home to go to camp in the summer. Though she seemed happiest when with her friends, she always disowned any wish to go to camp. Her ceaseless cheeriness made some people think of her as saccharin or superficial.

Having not grieved for his mother, John induces Peggy to conceal whining complaints, to embody the cherished smile, and not to leave him, even for the summer.

INVISIBLE LOYALTIES

The concept of invisible loyalties is described by Boszormenyi-Nagy and Spark as a moral dimension of human attachment. They assert that justice is a key motivator and determinant of family relationships. For those who cannot imagine justice to be a motivator, consider that the latency child says, "that's not fair" with a passion that appears to have the force of raw instinct. One effect of this force of justice is that our self-concepts and our family roles are shaped invisibly by whether we feel we received what was due to us and whether we feel we gave others what was due to them. Thus, we are driven by a sense of family justice. If we do not pay back our parents for what they did for us, then we may keep our books balanced by overpaying our children. People who feel they did not get what they deserved in childhood often "parentify" a child whom they expect will pay them back for the nurturance they missed.

Mary once said to John: "You think that people were put on earth to entertain you." John flatly denied it. He does, however, expect Peggy to be cheery. Peggy knows she is a constant buoy to her father. She sometimes says to herself, "My turn will come when I meet the right person and have children of my own."

BIRTH ORDER

Toman (1969) proposed that birth order affects one's marital and parenting behavior. A woman who has a younger brother is likely to have a better marriage with a man who has an older sister than with a man who has a younger brother. The families of origin trained the woman to relate to a younger male and trained the man to relate to an older female. Their roles would be familiar and complementary rather than unfamiliar and competitive.

Birth order is just one of many factors in role assignment. Various other theories show how children's roles and self-images are determined by their sex, the names they are given, whom they resemble, when they were born, etc.

OBJECT CHOICES

The most bedeviling aspect of our object choices is our tendency to select people who embody some features that we disown in ourselves. We do that partly to enjoy vicariously what we deny ourselves. We do it also in order to have a scapegoat: when a

forbidden part of us starts to surface, we can stimulate and intensify this feature in others and then attack it in them.

Everyone was mystified when Peggy started to date Luke, a bitter,
cynical young man. Peggy and Luke were talking after Peggy's father
had told her she could not go to a rock concert with Luke. At this moment
her father is walking toward them. Peggy and Luke whisper to each
other:

Peggy: Look what's walking our way.

Luke: Oh, it's the chimpanzee.

Peggy: You mean to say John, don't you?

Luke: You used to laugh when I called him chimp.

Peggy: (coldly) It is unnecessary to be disrespectful.

The complaining tones of John's mother, suppressed in Peggy, are
reintroduced to the family by Luke. At first Peggy vicariously
enjoyed his freedom to complain. Now she tends to stimulate his
sarcasm and then attack it.

THE INTERACTIONAL PERSPECTIVE

Concepts that bear on the interactional perspective are
nonhistorical. They clarify family conduct observable in the here
and now. Interactional concepts concern themselves principally
with *behavioral sequences* (what the family does) and with *family
structure* (a model that embodies the rules that govern these sequences).

A few definitions may help to introduce such interactional
concepts. If we call the family a system, then there may be several
subsystems, such as the parents, children, females, and males.
Each individual family member is also a subsystem. Various
terms may be used to describe the incidents and patterns of family interaction. Any single step in the interaction between family
members may be called a *move;* a train of two or more such moves
may be called a *sequence.* Some sequences are *cyclic.* The most
important sequences are those that are *recurrent.* Much is revealed about a family when we learn how each member
punctuates a given sequence, that is, which items of interaction
the family member notices. Consider the following cycle.

Move 1:   Peggy (starts to light a cigarette).
Move 2:   John (to Mary), "Can't you stop her from smoking so much?"
Move 3:   Mary (shouting at Peggy), "Your smoking is really disgusting!"
Move 4:   Peggy puts out cigarette.
Move 5:   John (to Mary), "You don't have to shout at her."
Move 6:   Mary (silent, looks vacantly into space).
Move 1:   Peggy starts to light a cigarette.

Father may regard his wife's shouting (move 3) as an isolated event and conclude that mother is needlessly harsh to Peggy. Peggy may take note of moves 5 and 6 and decide that mother is unable to speak up to father. Mother may notice the sequence of moves 1−5 and conclude that father undercuts her. The therapist needs to see beyond these individual punctuations to the full cyclic nature of the interaction.

Sequences are driven by obvious or obscure goals, targets or payoffs, and are governed by overt and covert family rules, roles, styles, etc. The rules of family interaction can be deduced from a careful study of its sequences. A family structure is a model that embodies all these rules. There are also *substructures* that delineate rules for particular parts of the family system.

DYSFUNCTIONAL COMMUNICATING MOVES

Satir (1967) defines four types of dysfunctional communication: *blaming, placating, distracting,* and *intellectualizing.* She adds one type of adaptive communication: *leveling.* These terms refer to moves made in family interactions. The more that family members employ dysfunctional moves, the more their sequences will be frustrating.

John: (making a blaming move) You women make Sundays dull.
Peggy: (making a placating move) I'll do something with you. (She turns off her favorite television show.)
Mary: (making a distracting move) Do they pick up rubbish on Lincoln's birthday?

Satir says that one reason people cannot level with each other is that they have defective self-esteem. They are sure that what they think, wish, or feel is bad and will be rejected by others.

PSYCHOPOLITICAL MOVES

Kantor (1975) has also made significant contributions to the understanding of moves and sequences. He describes four *psychopolitical positions*. In each move in a family sequence the family member acts either as an initiator, opposer, follower, or bystander. Families whose members stick inflexibly to one or another of these moves tend to be pathological.

DOUBLE BINDING SEQUENCES

The history of family therapy abounds with description and commentary upon all manner of dysfunctional sequences. We shall not dare to attempt to present a comprehensive list. We would, however, like to mention the double bind, which was originally suggested as an etiological factor in schizophrenia. Although Wynne (1976) and others document why the etiologic theory has lost favor, the double bind remains important because it shows us that we can delineate those elements in a sequence of communications that make it ambiguous, confounding, and potentially destructive. The central feature of the double bind is that it occurs when two simultaneous moves, each of a different type, give messages that are irreconcilable with one another. More important to the double bind idea, but less well known, are the additional demands that (1) there can be no discussion of the contradiction; (2) a response is required; and (3) there can be no escape from the situation.

TRIANGULAR SUBSTRUCTURES

One of Bowen's (1978) major concepts is triangulation. The triangle is a substructure; it maps the behavio. .f part of the family. The extended family is a chain of interlocking triangles. Bowen indicates that two people can escape conflict between them by forming a triangle.

John: You screw up everything. You are a whining, complaining drag.
Mary: I believe that you are having an affair with my sister.
John: That's crazy. You're out of your head.
Mary: I'm sorry, I don't know what made me say that. I sounded like that acidhead Luke.

John: I have no business calling you a whiner. When I compare you with creeps like Luke, I realize how totally unappreciative I am of all you've done.

John and Mary are not not in conflict, they are in collusion. When the link between them is troubled, they use Luke to create a triangle and spare each other by scapegoating him. Scapegoating is one kind of triangulation.

ELEMENTS OF FAMILY STRUCTURE

In addition to concepts that help us to understand moves, sequences, and substructures, there are ideas, notably those of Minuchin (1974) that offer us ways to grasp the structure of a whole family unit. In his theory the key elements of family structure are *hierarchies, boundaries, affiliations,* and *coalitions.* He provides symbols that help us map salient aspects of the family structure. Hierarchy is reflected by who is on top of the map. Boundary symbols indicate whether people interact too little (_____), too much (. . . . . .), or just enough (- - - - - -). Affiliation symbols represent attachments that are blocked (- - -/ - - -), overinvolved ($\equiv$), or just right (=). A coalition sign (}) indicates two against one.

If a clinician concludes that the heart of a problem is that father is overinvolved with daughter and that daughter has usurped mother's position in the family hierarchy, then he might map boundaries like this:

$$\frac{\text{Fa} \equiv \text{Dau}}{\text{Mo}}$$

They should be like this:

$$\frac{\text{Fa} \vdots \text{Mo}}{\text{Dau}}$$

The affiliations might be mapped like this:

$$\text{Fa} \equiv \text{Dau}$$
$$\text{Mo}$$

Or like this:

$$\left.\begin{array}{l} \text{Fa} \\ \\ \text{Dau} \end{array}\right\} \text{Mo}$$

They should be like this:

$$\begin{array}{c} \text{Fa} \;=\; \text{Mo} \\ \diagdown \quad \diagup \\ \text{Dau} \end{array}$$

These maps help us visualize the critical rules of family interaction.

The Experiential Perspective

Concepts associated with an experiential perspective relate to the subjective quality of an individual's experience in a family.

SELF-IMAGE

A familiar experiential concept from individual therapy is that of self-image. One can think of self-image as a kind of mug shot of oneself up against a neutral background. We suggest that a truer description of self-image is a brief movie of self in relationship to significant others against a background of meaningful detail. Thus, the mug shot version of self-image is but a subsection of a larger, more complex picture. Kantor (1975) proposes that we each have critical images that are easily accessible to our consciousness and that these images symbolize what family means to each of us.

DIFFERENTIATION

Bowen's (1978) notion of differentiation contributes to all the diagnostic perspectives. He describes well-differentiated (individuated) people as those who own up to their own thoughts and feelings, who tend to be autonomous and objective rather than dominated by emotional neediness and overreaction. From the experiential perspective, well-differentiated people can tolerate and enjoy experiences of intimacy and aloneness. Less differentiated people, when intimate, tend toward enmeshment (fusion) in which they eventually experience a terror of engulfment that impels them to take flight. When they are alone, they tend to suffer an unbearable sense of abandonment and long for fusion. (When undifferentiated people are seen from an interactional perspective their intimate relationships are usually characterized by cycles of enmeshment and flight.)

EMOTIONAL CLIMATE

Each family and each subsystem has its own climate, depending on its structure, the type of sequence currently in play, and who you ask: mother, daughter, father, or therapist. The language one might use to describe family climate is clearly limitless. For instance, if we ask John about his family climate on Sunday he might say it is "stale, monotonous, flat, cool, but flashy in spots." Not very appealing. However, it is not quite as terrible as family climates that have been described as airless, frozen, terrifying, paralyzing, and poisonous. During periods of enmeshment the climate between undifferentiated family members may be experienced initially as sublime, then explosive; at the peak of flight it may be experienced as frozen.

INNER EXPERIENCE

Fogarty (1976) states that a critical inner experience is a sense of emptiness that is part of the human condition. Emptiness is what we experience when confronted with the inevitability of our death, the hypocrisy of our values, or any of the other inevitable gaps between our perpetual illusions and the stark realities of life. Fused relationships may promise much but give us only illusory respite from emptiness. Actually no relationship can relieve us of it. No lover can make us immortal. The family therapist needs to distinguish this sense of emptiness from similar pathological experiences. Learning to bear normal emptiness is a key to individuation. Families must be relieved of the expectation that they can protect any member from this experience.

TREATMENT APPROACHES

Three treatment approaches will be described.

1. *Understanding.* The therapist interprets past influences and illuminates current patterns in order to enrich the family's knowledge about the origin and nature of its present predicament.
2. *Transformation.* The therapist strategically directs the family in order to modify and correct its dysfunctional moves, sequences, and structure.
3. *Identification.* The living model of the therapist and the active involvement of older family members promote new identifications and relax the grip of toxic introjects and destructive loyalties among family members.

We believe that the therapy of any particular family involves all of these approaches. Even if a therapist wanted to, he could not avoid providing some understanding, some direction, and some model for identification. Despite the inevitable blending of these approaches, we believe it is useful for us to examine each approach separately in order to make intelligible the complex array of techniques used in family therapy.

One reason for selecting the categories of understanding, transformation, and identification is that each of these approaches corresponds to each of the three ways people learn and change. People learn by increased knowledge, that is, by understanding; they learn by modification of behavior patterns, that is, by transformation; and they learn by imitation, that is, by identification.

In order to be effective, the techniques used in each of the approaches ought to conform to the principles which underlie the corresponding modes of learning. Therefore, in an approach based on understanding, the therapist would do well to be an engaging and lucid teacher; in an approach based on transformation, the therapist needs to pay vigilant attention to motivation, cooperation, and the contingencies of reward and punishment; in an approach based on identification, the therapist must attend to the kind of model he or she is setting for the family.

Loevinger (1971) notes that the three most prevalent approaches of child-rearing correspond to the ways people learn. Parents tend to rear children either by explanations, by directions and rewards, or by setting good examples. She also points out that no matter which learning theory guides the parent, the child may respond according to the principles of another learning theory. Thus, if a mother hits a boy for hitting his sister, the boy may hit her again despite his having been punished. He may do so because he is following his mother's example. So it is in all psychotherapy. The therapist may dispassionately aid the family in understanding the source and nature of its frozen intellectualizations but the family may learn only to identify with additional patterns of detachment modeled by their cool and distant therapist. It is therefore important for us to study not only each approach and the learning theory on which it is based, but also to examine the impact each approach may have according to the learning theory on which it is *not* based.

Earlier, three different diagnostic perspectives were explored. It is tempting, but misleading, to pair the perspectives with the approaches as follows: historical/understanding, interactional/transformation, and experiential/identification. Although it is true that exploring history may be necessary to help a family understand the origins of its misery, and an analysis of its interaction is critical to transforming its conduct, it is also true that one might want to study the pattern of its interaction to help a family understand it, or that one might want to study a family's history in order to design transformational directives that fit into family tradition.

Understanding

Techniques used in the understanding approach all have the objective of helping the family see what the therapist sees from each of the three perspectives. Thus, the goal of such a technique might be to help the family members grasp the way their behavior results from the flow of historical forces; it might be to help them learn the exact way their interactive sequences work to frustrate one another's needs; it might be to help them become aware of their own inner experience and that of other family members.

Family therapists have been enormously inventive in developing techniques for improving family understanding from all of the three perspectives. In order to shed light on family history, diaries, photo albums, taped interviews with relatives, even dramatic improvisations of past events have all been used. In the effort to teach families about their current interaction, family therapists may show families videotape playbacks of their behavior in therapy sessions. Family sculpting, drawing pictures of the family, and role playing have all been employed to help the family be aware of the quality of experience each member has inside the family.

Transformation

The techniques encompassed by the transformation approach involve activities directed or induced by the therapist and performed by one or more members of the family. The expected result of these tasks is to improve the nature of family interaction without necessarily increasing the family's understanding of itself.

Transformation techniques originate in a wide variety of psychotherapy schools including behavior modification, strategic psychotherapy, structural family therapy, communication-focused family therapy, Bowenian therapy, Gestalt therapy, psychodrama, transactional analysis, and others. Since many transformation techniques meet with considerable family resistance, some of their practitioners use subtle methods of obtaining client compliance such as those practiced by hypnotists like Milton Erickson (Haley, 1973, 1976).

OVERT DIRECTIVES

Transformation techniques involve directives that may be overt (straightforward) or convert (benevolently devious). An overt directive prescribes a task that directly benefits the family situation. Most directives are overt. They are usually aimed at moves, as opposed to sequences or structure. A family member may be instructed to improve the content of his communications:

Therapist: John, when you are ready, tell Mary exactly how you feel.

Or, he may be instructed to alter the style and language of his communications:

Therapist: John, when talking about feelings, try to start sentences with the word "I." Avoid telling Mary how *she* feels. If you want to know how she feels, *ask* her.

Sometimes straightforward directives are pointed at sequences:

Therapist: John and Mary, I want you both to listen to your daughter. Whenever she complains, I want you to thank her. Peggy, see if you can complain once in this meeting, but don't do it unless it feels safe.

Finally, overt directives may deal with structure:

Therapist: John, I think your wife and daughter have some things to talk over, woman-to-woman. Let's permit them to talk privately. Come here and tell me what happened in your visit to the urologist.

COVERT DIRECTIVES

A covert directive involves a task that may not be beneficial in itself, but is designed to lead indirectly to beneficial changes in family behavior and structure. For example, a couple who were having no sexual life were instructed to prepare a sumptuous dinner together. That activity led by analogy to other types of combined pleasure.

The paradoxical instruction is an important type of covert directive. If a defiant boy who fights continually with his sister is told to have ten fights with her in the following week, he might only have five. By prescribing the symptom of fighting, fighting loses its systems function: it is no longer defiant. A paradoxical instruction facilitates a change that might not occur if suggested openly.

Identification

In all family therapy, clients form new identifications and modify old ones through imitation of the therapist. In stranger-group therapy such changes in identification occur not only in relationship with the therapist but with the other clients as well.

In family therapy, family members may be even more powerful in affecting identifications than are therapists or other members of a stranger-group.

The potential for change in identification may be at its greatest when one shares therapy with one's parents, the most critical source of one's earliest identifications. It is tempting to believe that during interaction with our parents our identifications are most malleable—even long after childhood has past. Perhaps family loyalties play a role in this malleability. Our idea of what we are owed and what we owe others is inextricably woven into the fabric of our identifications. Much of this inner sense of expectation and obligation comes directly from the behavior and statements of our parents. If our parents originally helped us to establish our obligations, can they not also release us from them and thus help us modify this decisive aspect of our identifications?

CONCLUSION

We have outlined a scheme for classifying diagnostic theories and treatment approaches. We would like to conclude by suggesting how this scheme may be utilized.

Some students learn family therapy by studying separately each school of thought that currently prevails in the field. These schools are sometimes presented as though they bear no relationship to one another. The scheme we have developed provides the student with an additional way of learning about family systems and family therapy, one that facilitates comparing, contrasting, and integrating important elements in each school of thought. For example, a student using this scheme might notice that what one author calls a coalition, another author calls a triangle. The student will be in a position to see how they are the same and how they are different. He may try to integrate the concepts by applying triangle theory to coalitions.

For student and nonstudent, the scheme suggests interesting questions. What is the reason Dr. B cannot replicate the work of Dr. A? Is it because Dr. A's books reflect only the way she helps her families understand their histories, but does not describe the way her nonjudging, gentle method of exploration gives the family a humane model with which to identify? Perhaps Dr. A's lectures further mislead Dr. B. because Dr. A does not describe the way her style of interviewing subtly transforms family behavior by consistently rewarding family members when they listen carefully to each other and when they talk candidly about themselves. The scheme also raises questions about families that have been studied intensively from one perspective but not from others. We may wonder what kind of transgenerational history leads to families with anorexia that have been so carefully described from the interactional perspective. An answer to that question might give us clues about prevention. What about the therapists who use harsh techniques to alter locked-in systems? Do their clients identify with the harshness?

We could go on and on. Any system of classification has the potential of raising interesting questions. We are also aware that any system may also blind us to equally important issues. We hope readers will use this scheme when it promises to help them penetrate and clarify and put it aside when it appears to block and obscure.

REFERENCES

Boszormenyi-Nagy, I., & Spark, G. Invisible loyalties. Hagerstown, Harper & Row, 1973.

Bowen, M. Family therapy in clinical practice. New York, Jason Aronson, 1978.

Fogarty. T.F. On emptiness and closeness. *The Family*, 1973, *3(1)*, 3–12.

Freud, S. Mourning and melacholia. In Jones, E. (Ed.). Sigmund Freud, collected papers, volume 4. New York, Basic Books. 1959.

Haley, J. Uncommon therapy, The psychiatric techniques of Milton H. Erickson, M.D. New York, W.W. Norton & Co., 1973.

Haley, J. Problem solving therapy. San Francisco, Jossey-Bass, 1976.

Kantor, D. Inside the family. San Francisco, Jossey-Bass, 1975.

Loevinger, J. Patterns of parenthood as theories of learning. *In* Skolnick, A. and Skolnick, J.H. (Eds.). Family in transition. Boston, Little Brown & Co., 1971.

Minuchin, S. Families and family therapy. Cambridge, Harvard University Press, 1974.

Paul, N., & Paul, B. A marital puzzle. New York, W.W. Norton, 1975.

Satir, V. Conjoint family therapy. Palo Alto, Science and Behavior Books, 1967.

Satir, V. Peoplemaking. Palo Alto, Science and Behavior Books, 1972.

Toman, W. Family constellation. New York, Springer, 1969.

Wynne, L.C. On the anguish and creative passions of not escaping double binds: A reformulation. *In* Sluzki, C.E., & Ransom, D.S. (Eds.). The double bind: Foundations of the communication approaches to the family. New York, Grune and Stratton, 1976.

ADDITIONAL SOURCES

Guerin, P. (Ed.). Family theory and practice. New York, Gardner Press, 1976.

Napier, A., & Whitaker, C. The family crucible. New York, Harper & Row, 1978.

Papp, P. (Ed.). Family therapy: Full length case studies. New York, Gardner Press, 1977.

Robert M. Eisendrath, M.D.

2
The Borderline Patient: Individual Therapy from a Family Point of View

The interaction between family process, individual psycho-dynamics, and object-relations theory is nowhere clearer than in the treatment of those individuals who have been significantly damaged in growing up. These people, some of whom are borderline, have suffered what Winnicott (1953) has termed "environmental deficiencies." Often they are difficult patients to treat. Their distinctive psychopathology cannot be explained by classical psychoanalytic ideas of drive, ego distortion, or the conflict between intrapsychic agencies. (These of course exist in no lesser extent than in the classical neurotic.) Rather, they struggle with distortions created by pathological relationships that have taught them inadequate ways of satisfying their own needs and yearnings, and distorted styles of getting along with other people. In the broadest terms, this group includes the various character disorders, borderline personality disorders, and the psychotics.

THE BORDERS OF THE BORDERLINE CONCEPT

The scope of this chapter is limited to consideration of the borderline personality disorders. I believe that the issues of the psychotic patient are largely similar to those of the borderline—

intimacy versus distance, abandonment anxiety, and difficulties with the concept of self—and that, in fact, the prepsychotic frequently resembles the borderline patient. (Perhaps the differentiating factor between many borderline and psychotic patients is biochemical.) With severe stress, the psychotic patients suffer gross disintegration of thought and information processing, as in the case of schizophrenia, or governance of affect as in the manic depressives. The borderline problems are milder. It is hard to say where the boundary lies between borderline patients and "character disordered" patients. When you get to know the severe character disordered patients, they often seem like borderlines. As Kernberg (1977) has suggested, many are classifiable as borderline personality disorders.

Furthermore, I do not believe that the core issues for patients designated borderline are necessarily unique. Rather, like Winnicott's (1965) concepts of the true and false self, or narcissism as described by Kohut (1971), these issues are common problems. Moreover, family and psychodynamic issues are usually intimately intertwined. The patient who is only troubled by a neurosis and has totally resolved problems of the self, of early object-relation difficulties with the family, is hard to find.

The Range of the Concept

Since this chapter is not primarily a description of the borderline patients, let me define them only briefly. The people I am describing may range in overall life adjustment from the hospitalized, impulse ridden, dysphoric occupational or scholastic washout—the patients described in the studies of Gunderson & Singer (1975), Kernberg (1977), Perry & Klerman (1978), and others—to the successful colleague, political leader, or artist who has particular difficulties in close relationships and the management of love and hate—the patients described by Modell (1968), Guntrip (1969), Masterson (1976), and Winnicott (1965). Therapists treating this latter group frequently find that their original diagnosis of neurosis, with or without depression, fails to describe the complexity of their difficulties, which become increasingly apparent in long-term treatment. (Recently this latter group has been seen as "narcissistic character disorders.")

I believe the core problem common to this group is early abandonment anxiety, alternating with fears of engulfment, a result of traumatic early object experiences. Both of these anxieties, in turn, impair the development of a coherent sense of self and of ego stability, and engender a sense of rage and hatred directed at those seen as crucial to the individual's survival who have proven unreliable. Furthermore, there is a tendency to keep these opposite feelings isolated from each other.

DEFINING CHARACTERISTICS

The chief manifestations of this group are:

1. reliance on relationships with part-objects, with a marked degree of distancing required;
2. rapid and drastically alternating states of love and hate;
3. acting-out, particularly in the sexual area;
4. the presence of primary process without ego fragmentation;
5. heavy reliance on the defenses of projection, splitting, distortion, excessive idealization, and derogation;
6. transient and limited psychotic episodes under stress;
7. shifting and varied symptoms, referable to varied levels of "libidinal fixation";
8. a history of turmoil, confusion, frequent moves, losses, violence, or other major traumata. (In a clinic population the most common single historical event I have observed is alcoholic parents.)

The varied extent to which these factors are present makes this category appear to be something of a waste-basket classification.

Nobody knows why some people with terribly traumatic histories do so well in their lives. The conventional wisdom is that a few key positive personal influences have made the difference. Experience in intensive therapy and psychoanalysis supports that view; but our theory of positive experience lags well behind our theories of psychopathology and we are left with less to say about what we know matters so much.

LITERATURE REVIEW

The most helpful theoretical explanations of this group of patients have come from those English psychoanalysts taking an objects-relations point of view on development. They have asserted that object seeking is a primary force in human development.

Klein's Splitting Concept

Melanie Klein, whose work is usually cited as the first of the object-relations theorists, believed that the infant's relationship with the outer world is mediated by the formation of imagoes or internal object representations. These imagoes result from pain and frustration, but not necessarily that caused by external objects. What is internalized is produced by the *innate operation* of the infant's mind. For example, the imago of a part object, the breast, is internalized and then transformed (split) into "bad breast" or "good breast" by the mind of the child without regard to what any observer might be able to notice in the real relationship between the baby and the nursing mother. The imagoes are reacted to as though they are objects themselves. These imagoes, in turn, are the basis of the child's relationship to reality. These relationships may become too disturbing, however, and the inner objects then become too frightening to be used. Then, connection with the outer world may become attenuated. These split off or buried bad internal objects or imagoes remain relatively unmodified by real objects to remain governed by the primitive affects and fantasies.

Fairbairn: The Need for Relationship

Fairbairn (1952), the actual founder of the Object-Relations school, turned his attention to the split-off parts of a person's self, or the schizoid problem. Fairbairn thought that it is the relationship with the object and not gratification of impulse that is the ultimate aim of libidinal strivings. The deepest wish of all his patients, he concluded, was for a loving mother or father, and not for the quenching of a more limited instinctual tension. In keeping with this line, the main features of the schizoid patient are defenses against the painful affects of not being fully loved by a parent figure. The conflicts within the primary relationship of the infant to its mother lead to a splitting off of the relationship's intolerable aspects within the originally unitary ego.

Guntrip (1969) has further developed this thinking with his interest in this split-off self and its hidden relationships with old persecutory, hating internal objects. The job of treatment, he thought, was to uncover these painful internalized relationships and to attempt to replace them with new externalized and less punishing objects through the presence of the therapist.

Winnicott: The False Self

In a similar vein but with different words, Winnicott (1965) has focused on the same problem. For Winnicott, the split-off self would mostly correspond to what he would call the "true self." The "false self" is generated by the child's adaptation to a mother who is unable to relate accurately to the child's real needs. By and large, the patients with the most pathological false selves, persecutory imagoes, or split-off selves, are the borderline patients who are being discussed.

Winnicott (1953) has also contributed another useful concept, "the transitional object." In his own words, "the terms 'transitional object' and 'transitional phenomena' designate . . . the intermediate area of experience between the thumb and the teddy bear, [and] between oral erotism and true object relationship." Although what we usually think of as a transitional object, like a treasured special blanket or teddy bear, is in the world of real objects, it is imbued with magic or a special quality of the mother, that makes it more than a possession. Modell (1968) has speculated that the borderline is fixated at the transitional object stage of relating. When so fixated, the borderline views separation as a catastrophic loss of ties with the nurturing mother, and closeness as annihilating fusion with the destructive mother. Thus, he oscillates anxiously between the extremes, or is frozen, immobile, on the fence.

Relational and Communicational Views

Louis Hill (1955), among others, used the term "schizophrenogenic mother." He described these mothers as loving their children in a way which was "idealized, romantic and unrealistic and leads to the extreme denial of anything they observe in the child contrary to their fantasies." Wynne et al. (1958) wrote on "pseudomutuality in the family relations of schizophrenics." This concept essentially suggests that one ingredient in the families of schizophrenics (and I think borderline patients as well) is the demand for acceptance of a specific rigid role for a family member regardless of circumstances. There is a family ideology that must be maintained, even in the face of reality, at the risk of abandonment and exclusion. This pact of compliance with these roles is termed "pseudomutuality."

Other writers discussing the families of schizophrenic patients, who were in fact pioneers of family therapy, include Bateson, Jackson, et al. (1956), who presented the theory of a "double bind" between the patients and their families. This theory expressed the view that expectations within the families of schizophrenics were misleading, contradictory, and unresolvable because contradictions could not be acknowledged between messages at different levels. Whatever the designated patient did was wrong.

Lidz (1958) described "schism" and "skewing" present in the marriages of families with a schizophrenic member. This description again called attention to the inappropriate roles and expectations within the family, with behavior which beclouded, confused, and reversed what might be considered more normal expectations. What family therapists refer to as the "parenting child" may be an example of such skewed expectations, presented in a way which convinces the parenting child that he is in fact being parented.

Specific Studies of Borderlines

In the United States, several authors writing specifically on the borderline patient have made important contributions. Margaret Mahler has had a long and sustained interest in the evolution of borderline personality as part of childhood maldevelopment. She has outlined the phases of symbiosis and of separation-individuation, the task which the borderline has failed to negotiate (Mahler, 1975). She termed the particular time of this step of separation-individuation "sub phase rapprochement." Ordinarily it should occur between the 16th and 25th months of life. In the case of the borderline, the mother of this child is seen as libidinally unavailable to the child, who, having separated, returns to the mother for support and encouragement for this achievement. Her withdrawal punishes her child for separating. Thus, the child finds that separation has earned him vulnerability to abandonment and the anxiety attendant on this threat. In more normal development, the child's moves toward establishing a separate existence are rewarded by closeness and love during rapprochement.

Masterson (1976), who has been particularly interested in treating the adult borderline, has found considerable support for Mahler's views. He postulates that the intrapsychic result of these events is a splitting of the maternal and the self-representations. The split maternal part objects are the "withdrawing or aggressive-part unit" and "the rewarding or libidinal-part unit." He describes the former part-object representation of mother as "attacking, critical, hostile, angry, withdrawing supplies and approval in the face of assertiveness or other efforts toward separation-individuation." Chronic anger, frustration, and a feeling of abandonment and depression are associated affects. The part-self representation is negative—guilty and bad. The "rewarding maternal part object" supports regression and dependency; associated affect is positive and gratifies the wish for reunion. "The part-self representation" is a " good, passive, compliant child." He concludes by suggesting, "the task of therapy is to somehow help the patient see closeness and separateness as being compatible, and abandonment not the inevitable fate of love."

Zinner & Shapiro (1975), while at the NIMH, studied the family interactions of borderline and narcissistic characters. Their studies also showed that the parents of the patient reenact their own earlier fear of separation and behave as though the child's separation and autonomy were a rejection of themselves.

Sacrifice of autonomy is the price of continued admission into the family group. In accord with Winnicott, they reported, "The family cannot survive the emotional growth of the child."

Finally, Galdston (1978), in a paper presented at the 45th Anniversary Symposium of the Boston Psychoanalytic Institute, reported the findings of a ten-year study of child-abusing families. He noted that these families lived in a continual sado-masochistic struggle as a result of the unresolved issue of what he termed "oral aggression." They were unable to psychologically wean the infant and help it establish an independent or separate existence. He felt that the abuse resulted from the child's attempt to separate, which rekindled the rage of the parents who had themselves not achieved this stage. Although he did not specifically state it, I think Galdston's paper refers to families whose members show borderline personality organization.

GENERAL THERAPEUTIC CONSIDERATIONS

One of the central issues that the therapist must remain aware of is that these patients have lived lives in which reality has been distorted, feelings have been denied, and needs have been suppressed. What must have initially felt natural and necessary has been translated as being bad and/or unreal. I would like to illustrate what I think the emotional climate in these families is like by recalling parts from two movies, *Dr. Strangelove* and *Clockwork Orange,* both directed by Stanley Kubrick.

In a piece of black humor from the end of *Dr. Strangelove,* the world is blown to bits, as scenes of one atomic explosion after another, shot from different camera angles, are displayed to the accompanying music, "We'll meet again, don't know where, don't know when," a World War II-era song that is quite melodious and has a dance rhythm. A similar incongruent juxtaposition of music and action occurs in *Clockwork Orange,* when a group of men are shown running along, hitting people over the head, presumably killing them, while accompanied by the Fourth Movement of Beethoven's Ninth (Choral) Symphony, the "Ode to Joy." In both cases, the music and events being pictured communicate contradictory messages. In the movie, in small doses, the result is humorous. But as a constant life experience it leads to erosion of trust and a sense of reality. It promotes self-doubt, confusion, isolation, anxiety, and ultimately madness. The discordant messages raise questions about what is real. Is it what you see (or feel) or what you hear? Such discord systematically distorts a person's development. The growing child is essentially taught that its very existence, at least its separate existence, along with its separate perceptions, is wrong, bad, and ultimately will lead to its own destruction. Such children develop borderline disorders, or perhaps Winnicott's false self.

A further example of this split state, where one's own feelings and needs are inauthenticated, is provided by many of the stories of Joyce Carol Oates. She frequently describes the horror and terror of children buried in the silence of their internal worlds, forcing themselves to conform to crazy people around them in order to maintain contact, while losing contact with themselves. She uses frank violence in some of her stories. "Wonderland" (Oates, 1971) particularly emphasizes the overwhelming quality of alienation produced by an uncomprehending, reality-distorting environment which is part of the experience of this group of patients. In some ways, they are victims of a violent assault on their reality testing and their individuality.

SPECIFIC TREATMENT TECHNIQUES

The treatment follows from the trauma. It is to find the hidden self, to give up and mourn the old disappointing objects, to try to experience closeness without self-renunciation or destruction, and to find a reality in themselves denied by their family experience. In short, one important task of treatment is to join the right music or affect with the plot that has unfolded. The patient must begin to see the explosions and the blows with the true sound. This means stripping away the old myths of the family, the pseudomutuality, the double binds, the sado-masochistic interactions, the projections and distortions that have inauthenticated the patients' feelings of reality. Much of the work involves repeatedly reevaluating reports of family interactions, past and present. The same process applies to other current relationships, including the transference.

The therapeutic relationship provides the patient with a safe, stable, integrative context within which past experiences and the related self and object images can be reexperienced. Consentual validation is essential, as so few of the important facts of family life have ever been shared or even acknowledged. A therapist taking a neutral stance may inadvertantly mimic this pathogenic past. Unempathic remoteness must be avoided. The patient has already been treated as though his feelings were peculiar alienating forces unrelated to the world. To present a world different from that silent or distorting one of the past, the therapeutic relationship must be validating and collaborative. The therapist risks being sucked into traps and acting in a nontherapeutic way, and there is danger of being intrusive and controlling in order to avoid distance. This must be avoided too. What goes on between the patient and the therapist must be actively and repeatedly commented upon; the patient's tendency to see abandonment or co-option clarified; and the reality alliance affirmed.

Thus, I suggest a fair amount of activity, a considerable degree of personal openness and recognition of what is going on, promoting trust in the new reality of the therapeutic situation. With this safe and reliable context established, one must interpret, clarify, maintain one's own individuality and separation, and hear the rage that is attached to these split-off internal objects which made the patient feel so unlovable. With time, it is hoped that the grief from unloved parts of the self can be brought into the open and more satisfactory whole-object relations established. It is a very long and often painful process for both the patient and the therapist.

Use of Family Visits: Some Case Reports

I have tried to meet the members of the family when that is helpful, or to have the patient check with the family on points that have arisen in treatment. At times, therapy involves recurrent retesting of reality, as the patient checks with the family member(s) and then continues with new information or clearer delineation of the problem.

With one patient who had been in treatment for several years, I saw her mother for one visit after long preparatory work.

The patient had presented herself for treatment only because her daughter's problem was related to problems with the parents themselves. Her daughter, a vivid redhead with two younger brothers, became a holy terror at 12—tearing her clothes, biting her mother, wrecking her own room and possessions, refusing to go places. She claimed she couldn't walk and was carried by her mother. Her total rebellion so alarmed this proper Southern family that she was taken to a child psychiatrist, who at first thought she was borderline or schizophrenic. But she soon stopped all this after brief therapy as she found support for her emergent adolescent differentiation. Her mother knew nothing about relationships and was baffled. She became my patient only on the recommendation of her daughter's therapist, four years later, after her husband had been treated for depression. She claimed at first that her life was ideal in every other respect. I found her to be a compliant woman who required extensive suppression of her own inner life. The patient's mother had done the same thing with *her* mother. The patient's daughter had rebelled, which started the sequence leading to treatment.

Treatment took a long time to get past her defensive blandness and unrevealing sociable propriety. When her defenses eventually relaxed, a picture of her father emerged as emotionally absent. He was a successful corporate lawyer who travelled a lot and, when home, needed a lot of time alone in his study to prepare his reports. He was admired and respected by his clients. My patient adored him uncritically. On reflection, she realized he was a distant man who had no truly personal relationships.

As she became more personally expressive, she began to object to my desk, which was not as neat as her father's. She struggled to maintain her idealizations while beginning to respond to me as I am. As she made tentative attempts towards personal relating, I shared aspects of myself and my family experiences with her, which fostered trust in a relationship that was genuinely personal, not merely formal and correct.

During treatment the patient brought in a photo of herself at age two, sitting on her mother's lap while two older siblings stood alongside. The father was not in the picture. The mother was absolutely beautiful, resembling a Gibson Girl, but she looked overwhelmed and anxious and was not touching the patient at all. It became clear that this mother had only survived without her husband's help by using compliance with superficial norms. The patient had preserved what little rebellion was left by a brilliant performance as a successful and dutiful daughter. After we had discussed all of this and the superficiality of the relationship with her mother, with whom she really felt very uncomfortable, the mother came in for one hour. This woman, who was lovely in the 45-year-old picture was now in her mid-70s and was a well dressed, well preserved grandmother. She immediately opened up without a pause, talking of her own problems—trying to be a good parent and helper to her daughter—as well as speaking of her love for the patient and her views of the patient's problems. I was quite moved at the obvious good will and the attempt to be helpful. At the beginning of the next hour, however, the patient simply stated, "My mother doesn't know who I am." Her mother's image of her was her own fiction. This was the summation of several years of work and the music that fit the words in her life. Ultimately, it freed her up to be closer to her own family and experience her own feelings.

Another patient presented as being much sicker, with hallucinations and increasing incapacity and isolation. She had been given a leave of absence from her law school. She spoke of herself in the third person. She slept with four lights on at night lest one of them burn out leaving her in the dark. She had frequent intermittent periods of brief psychosis. This was a particularly long treatment, which included clarification of the family dynamics. She was the third child of a dissolving marriage and had been totally rejected by her father, whom she had adored. After the divorce, both parents remarried, but she never saw her own father.

As the story unfolded, she recalled overhearing, at the age of five, her mother telling her father that the patient was not his child, but rather the child of the man the mother subsequently married. Later it became clear that her mother's statement was not true, that the mother merged fact and fantasy without discrimination. Her mother would psychologically merge herself with the patient whenever the mother envied or needed her. Her mother would abandon her whenever the mother felt competitive or feared the patient's growth of autonomy; she fitted the classical description of a "schizophrenogenic mother."

After many unsuccessful attempts and lengthy discussion in

therapy, the patient had a rapprochement with her father. We explored the effect of mother's lie upon father, and then father's difficulty with closeness himself. She spoke to her father about this. She could not do this before she had been able to claim me as a surrogate parent, however. Ultimately, the patient was able to separate from her mother, get to be a friend with her long-lost father, and mourn the horror of her upbringing. She accomplished this by our consistent review of the family interactions; by long periods of understanding her pain, her fears, and her defenses; and by my constant interpretation of the transference. All were necessary for her to achieve a separation and end treatment. Her summation of treatment was that it had been her upbringing and that I had been a mother and a father to her.

There are more clinical examples that might be given: the attempt at repairing the damage done by a dying mother's constant tripping on LSD in order to avoid the pain of her own death, with her daughter, the patient, who was 13 at the time that this had occurred; the use of old family letters and reports of siblings to confront the reality of a loved father who was also paranoid, sadistic, and rejecting. All illustrate the point that these patients' relationships with their families, past and present, are central themes. Anything that leads to the examination of these difficult relationships is useful.

CONCLUSION: DEVELOPING COHERENCE AND AUTHENTICITY

I have discussed how considerations of the family fit into the individual therapy of borderline individuals. The family has played a major role in providing the borderline patient with distorted views of self, of other people, and of relationships. Both the patient's family relationships and his internal dynamics must be addressed. I have emphasized one aspect of this problem, the attempt to link appropriate affects with past and present events to foster the patient's developing sense of authenticity as these feelings and events become congruent.

I have indicated the importance of the therapeutic context. This is crucial to all patients, but particularly so to this group. Therapy itself must provide the patient with a useful model for personal growth. It must not inadvertently mimic the relationships of the past.

REFERENCES

Bateson, G., Jackson, D., Haley, J., and Weakland, J. Toward a Theory of Schizophrenia. *Behavioral Science,* 1956, *1,* 251–264.

Fairbairn, W.R.D. Psychoanalytic studies of the personality. London, Tavistock Publications, 1952.

Galdston, R. *Violence in the family.* Talk presented at the 45th Anniversary Symposium of the Boston Psychoanalytic Institute and Society on "The Violent Individual," 1978.

Gunderson, J.G., Singer, M.T. Defining Borderline Patients: An Overview. *American Journal of Psychiatry,* 1975, *132,* 1–10.

Guntrip, H. Schizoid phenomena, object relations and the self. New York, International University Press, 1969.

Hill, L.B. Psychotherapeutic intervention in schizophrenia. Chicago, University of Chicago Press, 1955.

Kernberg, O.F. Borderline conditions and pathological narcissism. New York, Jason Aronson, 1977.

Klein, M. Envy and gratitude: A study of unconscious sources. London, Tavistock Pub Ltd; New York, Basic Books, 1957.

Kohut, H. Analysis of the self. New York, International University Press, 1971.

Lidz, T. Schizophrenia and the family. *Psychiatry,* 1958, *21,* 21–27.

Modell, A. H. Object love and reality. New York, International University Press, 1968.

Mahler, M.D. The psychological birth of the human infant. New York, Basic Books, 1975.

Masterson, J.F. Psychotherapy of the borderline adult. New York, Brunner/Mazel, 1976.

Oates, J.C. Wonderland. Greenwich, Fawcett Crest Books, 1971.

Perry, J. C., & Klerman, G.L. The Borderline Patient. *Archives of General Psychiatry,* 1978, *35,* 141–150.

Sutherland, J.D. Objects Relations Theory and the Conceptual Model of Psychoanalysis. *British Journal of Medical Psychology,* 1963, *36,* 109–18.

Winnicott, D.W. Ego distortion in terms of the true and false self. In Winnicott's Maturational processes and the facilitating environment. New York, International University Press, 1965.

Winnicott, D.W. Transitional Objects and Transitional Phenomena. *International Journal of Psychoanalysis,* 1953, *34,* 89–97.

Wynne, L.D., Ryckoff, I.M., Day, J., & Kirsch, S.I. Pseudomutuality in the Family Relations of Schizophrenics. *Psychiatry,* 1958, *21,* 205–20.

Zinner, J., & Shapiro, E.R. Splitting in families of borderline adolescents. In Mack, J.E. (Ed.) Borderline states in psychiatry, New York, Grune & Stratton, 1975.

Larry H. Strasburger, M.D.

3
A Case of Post-Partum Depression:
Individual and Family Treatment

I would like to ask you to imagine joining me in a special place, to come into the office where I work every day. The room is a quiet one, enclosing an atmosphere of stability and constancy. On the walls are some pictures which I enjoy, and there are some familiar objects about that, like old shoes, I know well and am comfortable with. Come in and sit quietly with me while I meet with two people. I'd like you to be empathic both with them and with me and to join in the encounter, if you will. As you participate in our meeting, you can share some of the feelings and thoughts evoked in each of us while we are together.

Why do I invite you to join me? I do it for several reasons. I would like to share my experience in the hope that it may be helpful to others doing individual and couple psychotherapy. I would like to show that in individual psychotherapy the person being treated exists in a context, a family context, that should not be ignored. I would like to demonstrate how some of the ways an individual relates to others (that existential stuff of individual therapy) can be thrown into high relief through family interviews. Finally, I would like to illustrate the way in which a family therapist may employ a variety of techniques in his work with a single family. We have a rich armamentarium of approaches which, if flexibly used, can bring an experience of many-faceted discovery.

33

In this story you will hear about my work with Elly, the identified patient. Then you will hear about my work with Elly and her husband Patrick, together, and you will hear about the outcome of using these techniques. I hope that I can demonstrate some of the complementarities of individual and family treatment. I also hope to show some of the complementarities between an individual and a couple's behavioral dynamics, wherein the individual's personal traits are interwoven with the transactions of the couple.

THE IDENTIFIED PATIENT

Elly was a slender, attractive woman in her early thirties who came to me because she had heard from a friend that I might be helpful. She had been upset, suffering from severe feelings of depression subsequent to the birth of her first child. Her son was about nine months old at the time of our first meeting. She had the classical signs of depression, with feelings of black despair and thoughts that she might kill herself. On her way to and from our first meetings she considered driving her car into an abutment, thinking that it would appear to have been an accident. She was also having trouble with her baby, who seemed irritable and could not be gotten onto a regular sleep schedule. She was having a difficult time and I sympathized with her.

She and her husband had been married shortly after she had had surgery for a gynecological problem, and their sexual relations had been difficult. They had wanted a child and had intentionally conceived. She was frightened whether or not she could be a good mother. In addition to her own worries about her adequacy, she felt pressure from her husband to be perfect. He seemed to her to want a pregnancy which he could show off to his colleagues, enhancing his own pride. She felt on public display. When they attended classes in natural childbirth together, she felt that his investment in the process was even greater than her own. She was extremely upset when the child had to be born by Caesarean section. She was disappointed in herself and felt like a failure. She thought that she had let her husband down. She felt confirmed in her sense that she was not a good mother.

A few weeks after the birth of the baby, she discovered a

lump in one breast. She went to a surgeon who told her she had
cancer, then retracted his statement—maybe she did not have
cancer. She was terrified. She went to surgery unsure whether
she would die and leave her new baby or simply be faced with a
loss of the breast and permanent disfigurement. She feared being
unable to care for the baby due to mastectomy. She was relieved
when the mass turned out to be benign.

Her fears and sense of inadequacy had been painful, but
worse than these had been the sense that she was increasingly cut
off from her husband. This alienation was worsened when he
received the business promotion that he had been hoping for. His
new job meant that he would have independence, executive responsibility, and much more money. The new job, however, meant
moving to another city. Without a great deal of consultation between the two of them, he accepted it. Abruptly, they were split
up for five days a week while he commuted by plane and she
remained at home.

After several months of intermittent separation, Elly herself
moved to the new city. She lived in a hotel for several months
with the new baby, her husband gone long hours at the new job
where he was trying to prove himself. The burden of taking care
of her new child, the recovery from surgery, and the emotional
trauma of the threatened loss by surgery were difficult to bear. In
addition to these, the friendlessness and anonymity of life in a
new city were very painful. She missed her friends and family
home. She felt overwhelmed, helpless, and estranged from her
husband. She thought she couldn't cope with the responsibilities
of motherhood. Helplessly, she tried to conceal her feelings from
her husband because she felt they angered him. He seemed en-
thusiastically caught up in his new job, and appeared to have
little patience with her anxieties. For him, this time was the
chance of a lifetime. His pinnacle was her nadir.

During our initial meetings she looked helplessly to me for
assistance. She was warm and engaging. There was an appealing
vagueness to her manner that always seemed to imply more than
I was ever able to touch. I had the sense that if I were sensitive,
empathic, I would engage with an unusual person. I liked her and
wanted to be helpful; at the same time, I was intensely frustrated;
I always seemed to be just on the verge of being able to understand something that would be useful to her, but never quite

managed it. She seemed to want something from me that I felt I should be able to supply, but couldn't quite.

I tried to help her to understand that the pregnancy, the surgery, and the dislocation were important milestones that must inevitably bring strong emotional responses. To expect herself not to react was unrealistic. I tried to encourage her to be accepting of her own feelings and not to expect herself not to be effected by these major events in her life. In this, I think I was successful. She later said that our work together validated her feelings, and this was important to her.

There were difficulties in therapy. I could not get a purchase on the transference; it seemed ephemeral, elusive. I tried to listen harder. I encouraged her to come more often, hoping that increased intensity would facilitate the work. She said that she could not, however, because her husband opposed her having therapy at all and she did not want to anger him still further. He thought it a disgrace to have a wife in psychotherapy. Frequently I felt I was straining to understand her. What I needed to know seemed just a little beyond my reach. In my frustration I began to react in ways I didn't like in myself. There were interviews in which I became increasingly sleepy. I wasn't bored, but I was fatigued. I was not retreating from anything that I was consciously aware of in the relationship, but I was aware that I was not able to be my best self as a therapist. It seemed as though we were marking time. She frequently frustrated my attempts to learn more by vagueness, by half-articulated thoughts that never came home, by trailing off after half-sentences. I felt confused, unable to understand what was needed, and handicapped by something that I could not grasp. Later on, she said of this time, "I felt isolated, like a child who has no children on the street to play with but won't go to the next block where there are lots of kids to play, due to shyness."

Background

Elly had grown up an only child in a Jewish family in a large middle-western city. Her father had come from Central Europe where he and his family had been the victims of religious persecution. She recalled his stories of being chased terrified through the streets of his town pursued by people with sticks throwing rocks at him. Although saddled by poverty, he was a vigorous man who worked, saved his money, and went to high school, college, and law school at night. He supported his three sisters, who were competitive, critical women. When he married, he chose a wife who was quite unlike them. Elly's mother was very attractive and a good deal younger than her father. She was very shy and did not share his interest in social and political issues. He often wanted to go out at night to attend artistic functions, but she rarely joined him. Elly's mother generally tried to avoid arguments and, when cornered, always broke down and cried. Her mother's sense of the world was that it was a dangerous place where a person could get hurt, while her father's was that it was a place to be mastered. She carefully protected Elly and insulated her from what she saw as a hostile environment. Her father was busy in his legal practice, frequently unavailable till late at night. Much of his earnings went to support his sisters as well as his own family. Despite his vigor he was paralyzed by recurrent depressions. The family considered these to be disgraceful and concealed them. When she was about eleven, he made a suicide attempt, taking sleeping pills. He was discovered and hospitalized. Relatives were told that he had gone away on vacation. Another severe depressive episode occurred during Elly's late adolescence, and shortly after this her father died of a heart attack.

Elly was not allowed to go away to college despite her wishes to do so. Her parents wanted her close by, and she sensed their fear that she might become sexually active were she to be away from home. During her late adolescence she began to show some artistic talent, and she utilized this to obtain her first job with a creative professional person. Here she was able to exercise her aesthetic talents, as well as her organizational skills. At the same time, she pursued her own artistic interests. She was a skillful weaver, though she frequently bogged down in the middle of work and had trouble completing it. Two years after college she married as an escape from the responsibilities of work and having to fend for herself. She was excited by her husband's facility with words, his aggressive personal domination of the sphere around him, and his personal charm and good looks. She felt at the same time that she had much to give him through her own sensitivity. She felt that they had been happy together up until the birth of their first child.

Working in psychotherapy, as noted, led to our mutually feeling "stuck." Recognizing our impasse in psychotherapy, I suggested that, as it was not possible for us to meet more often, some alteration of the format of treatment was essential. Although she said that her depression was much improved, she wanted something more from the psychotherapy. I shared the feeling that there was more to be gained. I suggested that she bring her husband with her, hoping that this might break the impasse which we had experienced. Many of the difficulties that she was now describing seemed to center around her relationship with him, and I hoped that with his perspective we could unlock this frustrating and incomplete therapeutic situation.

THE SPOUSE

Pat was an articulate, charming man. He was dramatic in manner and spoke with a sonorous bass voice which conveyed great decisiveness. He came to the meetings with his wife reluctantly. Although he exuded an air of optimism and certainty, he was obviously afraid to examine his role in the marriage.

Although currently in touch with his parents, he was estranged from his mother. The family had been the only Jews in a small Connecticut town where his parents' method of assimilation, especially fostered by his mother, had been to become more Yankee than the villagers themselves. Mother inculcated Pat with Yankee virtues: stoicism, pride, suppression of feeling, and a respect for education. Pat was taken to artistic and cultural events from a very early age. He described his parents as "a coconspiracy of two scared people who dreamed a dream of fulfilling themselves through their children's education." Pat's father had come from Russia as a child, a second son whose parents had never learned English following their immigration. He was a logical, orderly man who was affectionate yet tended to retreat from his wife during her emotional outbursts. Occasionally he got excited and enthusiastic about business ventures, always to be reined in by his wife, who thought him "unseemly." He was not, in his son's eyes, a model of success. Pat's mother also came from an immigrant family, although she was born in this country. She was described as stand-offish, steely, and ironic. Externalizing her own terror of being an initiator, a mover, a risker, she could be ruthless in her put-downs and criticisms of her husband as weak and lacking ambition. Pat described her as "a woman with an archistic, wild, loony side, as well as a fear of responsibility." Although close to his mother as a small child, Pat felt wary and fearful of her because of her internal contradictions and her frightening attacks on his father. By the time of his marriage he had cut himself off from her.

In adolescence, Pat was not rebellious, but rather sought his parents approval. Instinctively shy, he mastered a "life of the party" stance. His skill as a musician was a great social advantage. Slow to mature in his relationships with women, he felt he had to be a strong man in order to please, but at the same time was wary and skeptical. As the years passed, he was increasingly embarrassed about his lack of sexual experience. After college, once in the business world, his shyness with women began to build on itself, and he had great difficulty making any kind of sexual advances. One of the things that attracted him to his future wife was his fantasy that she was a sexually experienced woman. He looked to her to educate him. Unlike his mother, she seemed to be stable, direct, and "hidden but warm." Success in the business world was extremely important to him, even more important to him than relationships, even though success might mean loss of connectedness with his family of origin and with his wife as well. He felt conflict about this. Of his parents, he said, "If I hadn't come home an alien through success they would have been displeased, unhappy, and disappointed in me." The displacement of these values into his relationship with his wife made problems for the two of them.

THE COUPLE WORK: TECHNIQUES

This was a picture-book couple. He was handsome and she was lovely—he, articulate, gregarious, decisive; she, graceful, artistic, charming. The initial task of the couple work was to win his confidence. He had come into a long-standing therapeutic relationship, a difficult position. He could have felt excluded, a third party. He could easily have been scapegoated. Initially, I focused strongly on trying to understand his side of issues while not losing touch with her. I had to pay special attention to his feeling like a fifth wheel, an unnecessary adjunct. As I showed myself both interested in his point of view and receptive to his style of presentation, he developed confidence in my impartiality. I tried to teach both of them that I could indeed be on both sides at once, appreciating the validity of both of their points of view, even when they differed. I was quite structured, shifting from the rather nondirective role that I had taken with Elly into a role in which I actively took control of the meetings. I listened for the issues of the moment, encouraged each of them in turn to speak. I controlled the access to the floor of the forum. After one spoke, I would then turn to the other and say, "What do you think about this?" I attempted to limit the vocabulary to cognitive terms and toned down the use of emotional terms. They were very angry with one another, at times so angry that I feared they couldn't do any work together. The cognitive vocabulary—"thinking" rather than "feeling"—was deliberating chosen in order to reduce this anger.

Taking control was essential to block Pat's attempts to control the floor. With the shift of competence in the marriage, Elly looked to him to provide direction and moderation for their discourse. She invited him to tell her what was valid and what was not. His acceptance of these invitations, of course, led to her feeling intruded upon, devalued, and enraged. I emphasized that each must speak only for himself or herself. I encouraged them to speak to me rather than to each other. I broke in at points where attributions were being made. I both intervened directly with the person who was speaking and also with the other, saying, "Why are you letting him speak for you? Why are you encouraging him/her to voice *your* thoughts?" I attempted to promote their listening to one another, as well to promote each individual's self-observation.

Back to Back

One of the early problems I encountered was the way each carefully scrutinized the other for signs of approval or disapproval. This heightened their emotional reactivity and often led one to interrupt the other's statements. They frequently cued each other with the shift of an eyebrow or minute gesture of a hand as to whether a statement was acceptable or nonacceptable, substantially inhibiting exchange. As I became aware of this, I required them to turn their chairs so that they would have their backs to each other, though both could turn sideways and see me. This felt quite awkward at first. Soon, however, freed from the necessity to scan each other constantly, and from the fear of external criticism, they began to be much more open with personal expressions of feelings and wishes. Out of view and unable to see the other, the focus of each turned more inward. Some of the excessive niceness and placating fell away and they became much more authentic. It was many weeks until I became convinced that the two could turn back to face one another and still function with one good eye turned inward. When difficulties with cueing occurred again, I again separated them for short periods. During these times, I continued to encourage them to speak to me rather than to each other.

Role Playing

One of the most difficult times for this couple occurred at the end of the work day. Pat tended to come from the office feeling quite expended and wanting to withdraw. She, deprived of social contact all day, wanted to engage; frequently fights began. He felt that he had done his bit for the day by working in the office; she wanted help with the domestic chores. Often fights centered around whether he would pay attention to their young child, or whether the child would simply be put to bed so Pat could have some peace. I encouraged them to role play this scenario over and over again. It seemed cruel to push them into this situation, but I wanted to magnify it and throw it into high relief. Initially each played his own part. Then I filled in for one partner or the other. It became easier for the partner who stood aside to hear the other's position in the discourse. Finally, I suggested a role reversal, wherein I played the part of the husband and required Pat to play his wife's part. This was repeated with Elly. I attempted to deliberately exaggerate the position, acknowledging to them I was doing this for didactic purposes. Most difficult of all for them, I asked them to reverse roles, each playing the other. Pat gradually came to realize how his requests that his wife play the role of handmaiden to his needs were humiliating. At the same time,

Elly became increasingly aware of her petulance, and self-centered insistence that she have reparations for all the deprivation that she had suffered during the day. The affective results of the role-play were a markedly decreased tension in the office visits as well as fewer fights at home.

Doubling or Coaching—Technique Borrowed from *Psychodrama* (Yablonsky, 1976)

Frequently during the role play, and later on during other transactions, I rose from my chair to stand behind the individual who was speaking, acknowledging while doing so that I was going to act as a double, or as a coach. From behind the individual, with one hand on his shoulder, I restated the words that he had stated, trying to clarify or to extend them. By my physically, as well as emotionally, identifying with the speaker, his emotional expression was facilitated. His feeling understood and sense of alliance were enhanced. A dimension was added, and feelings that were difficult to verbalize could be expressed. It was also an education in stating one's own case. I encouraged the person whom I was doubling to restate my statement of his position. This left substantial freedom to the individual to use what I had to say if it was helpful and to discard it if it was not.

The Letter (Sacks, 1974)

With gradual realization that some of the difficulties being experienced in the relationship were a recapitulation of old feelings of Elly toward her father, I encouraged her to pretend to write a letter to him. In the letter she was able to speak dramatically to his desertion of her during childhood during his active involvement in his own work. As she spoke her emotions rose. She began increasingly to express a recognition of his caring, both for her and her mother and for the other women in his life as well—his three sisters. As the letter expanded, covering her adolescent years, she began to talk to her dead father about his suicide attempt. She expressed an understanding for the great pressures that he experienced, for his self-criticism, for his efforts to go beyond himself in caring for others. She had never been able to tell him this during his lifetime. The letter called forth many tears, as well as a new understanding of her father's generosity. She realized, in some ways for the first time, how much he had cared about her and how much she had meant to him. Her feelings were very sympathetically reflected by her husband, who acted as a double for her. She was able to recognize and better appreciate many of her husband's efforts on her behalf, and her anger toward Pat diminished.

Parental Reversals (Friedman, 1977)

In the process of exploring family relationships, I encouraged each of them to imagine a marriage between Pat's father and Elly's mother and then one between his mother and her father. A discussion of these fantasied marriages and an attempt to explore what it would be like to be a child in each one, clarified many parental attitudes and the reactions that these provoked. Individual value systems were better defined as these differences were sharpened. A great deal of sympathy was evoked for all four parents. Each person became more aware of separate issues involving individual parents, whereas there had been a tendency to regard parents as a merged unit, en bloc.

Reframing (Watslawick, et al., 1974)

Changing the conceptual or emotional setting of a transaction to an alternative that also fits the facts may profoundly alter the meaning of a transaction. Thus, it was often helpful to the couple for me to intervene by taking a particular behavioral sequence out of its context and offering a new interpretation of it. For example, at one point late in the treatment, Pat was unhappy because he felt that his wife needed him less than she formerly did. He felt that in some ways she was distancing herself from him as she had in the past. As her double, I reframed this. I told him, speaking for her, "You, Pat, have been affirming for me in a way that has enhanced my self-esteem so that I no longer feel so desperately grabby." This transformation offered a view of the situation which was substantially less painful. As Epictetus said, "It is not the things themselves which trouble us, but the opinions that we have about these things."

Clarification

I tried to clarify differences in style that existed between the two, particularly differences in dealing with new information. These differences were not necessarily divisive unless they were regarded by the couple as differences in substance. Often, however, the two reacted to each other's style without hearing the content. This could lead to an apparent polarization that interfered with the couple's problem-solving capacity. Frequently she approached a matter skeptically, hesitantly, and with many reservations; his tendency was to plunge boldly in and to accept something whole-hog without question. He was interested in the new; she was interested in retaining the old. Each individual was better able to tolerate the other's style when it was clear that they were in agreement regarding substance or content.

As well as clarifying style differences, I attempted to clarify defenses with each of them. Each tended to use the other to defend against the helplessness of needing and wanting. In addition, her tendency to use him as initiator, or as executive ego, often made it difficult for him to understand her particular position. These defensive strategies were clarified repeatedly in different contexts.

Pursuit and Distance (Fogarty, 1976)

This style for the regulation and management of personal boundaries often tends to resolve itself as the couple achieves a better sense of self–other differentiation. As the recognition and acceptance of personal differences grows, a parallel growth of confidence in the integrity of one's own boundaries occurs. As intrusion or abandonment become less threatening to the individuals, pursuit and distance become less of an issue for the couple. The therapist, however, can also work directly with the symptomatic interpersonal transaction.

In working with this couple, I tried to deal actively with the pursuer and to leave the distancer alone. This followed the theory that the distancer probably cannot be reached and the pursuer is the only accessible party. The pursuer needs to face his emptiness, and the distancer must confront his loneliness. When the pursuer takes a lesson from his partner and learns to distance himself a bit, with the help of the therapist, the distancer often halts his flight.

Direct Suggestion

I utilized some direct suggestions with the couple, for example, in suggesting procedures to be followed with their child. She seemed very reluctant to set limits or to establish a schedule for him other than that which emanated from him. I also suggested when we were talking about their sexual relationship, that they try to have intercourse at a time when each of them was not as fatigued as they were at night.

Prescription of the Symptom

One of the difficulties that had been plaguing their sexual relationship was her tendency to "turn off," as she called it. She would involuntarily, apparently, lose all sexual feelings during the process of intercourse. I encouraged her to take command of this symptom by deliberately inducing it in herself early in their love-making, to intentionally turn off. As she tried this, she found that she could turn off deliberately during love-making. After she tried it for a while, allowing the process to go farther and farther toward a satisfactory union, she began to feel that she had developed a control that she had not had before, and this difficulty became less troublesome.

RESULT OF THE COUPLE THERAPY:
WHAT WAS ACCOMPLISHED

During the couple therapy, Elly's depression continued to diminish. Her vagueness, alienation, and sense of inadequacy markedly improved. She said that she was more comfortable and more accepting of her feelings. She developed a confidence in dealing with her husband that she would not have gotten alone. She learned about him personally, and learned to be more sensitive to him. She became constructively aware that she had been expecting satisfaction and happiness from another person, though it was her responsibility to achieve these things for herself. She had regarded marriage as a panacea for all her ills and had been using it to escape responsibilities. She realized she had hidden behind her husband's personality to alleviate her fears of people.

Despite the changes, some problems remained; everything wasn't rosy. I was aware that she could still be vague and could expect me to function as a synthetic part of herself. It was also clear that she still had many fears that were not adequately dealt with. She still feared loss of control; she still feared personal fragmentation. There would probably never be a total alleviation of the physical pain that she experienced due to the unsuccessful gynecological surgery.

Her identification with her father, her fear that she would be like him, with his depression, his suicide attempt, and his elec-troconvulsive treatments, was substantially resolved. She had shifted in her position with regard to her husband and was much more able to take initiative at the close of the couple treatment. She was no longer stuck in the role of "follower" or "opposer." She had become able to listen, rather than simply to argue with her husband. Her misinterpretations of his feelings diminished. The discussion of her husband's sexual difficulties helped her to un-derstand that she was not sole owner of the problem. She felt that she had been able to be genuinely helpful to him and he felt the same way.

Pat felt much less troubled about the marriage. He was no longer so frightened of divorce. He no longer had the sense of guilt that he had failed his wife and not been there when she needed him. He felt closer to her and more able to understand her feel-ings. He felt able to disagree with her and yet, at the same time, better able to understand her. He felt that his own sympathetic capacities had been enhanced by the treatment. He felt that he had a new appreciation for Elly as an individual in her own right; he began to appreciate her unique form of eloquence. He was painfully aware of his sexist feelings, that he had required a slave in his wife. Although he did not like seeing this in himself, he felt it was most useful to become aware of it. He discovered that many of her demands on him were actually quite achievable requests. He felt that exploration of his own family relationships had been extremely useful and had helped him to draw nearer to his own parents and brother.

THEORETICAL CONSIDERATIONS

In treating this couple I relied primarily upon four theoreti-cal models. I relied on a psychodynamic model, a structural model drawn from Munuchin (1974), a model drawn from Kantor & Lehr (1975), and a model based on Bowen (1978).

From a psychodynamic point of view in the individual work, I followed the precepts of Beck (1967) in dealing with depression. I tried to deal with feelings of learned helplessness. I was influenced by Jerome Frank's ideas that successful psychotherapy helps people cope with feelings of demoralization (Frank, 1974). From an object relations point of view, when Elly stopped using Patrick for her synthetic ego functions her envy and anger toward him diminished, and she was able to deal with him without distancing him. She no longer needed to hide behind someone to escape responsibility and then blame him for dominating her. Her new ability to state her own position altered the relationship that so frustrated Patrick through its ambiguity.

Elly's closeness to her son and her distance from her husband suggested a family structure outlined by Minuchin. Here, as the father becomes more and more peripheral to the family, the family becomes increasingly disabled. The Minuchin model dictated bringing the husband into treatment, a structural move. As a result of directly making the husband a more central figure, the marriage worked better. Each individual's experience became changed through an alteration in his social context.

Kantor and Lehr's four-player system, with its roles of mover, follower, opposer, and bystander, was another useful conceptual framework for understanding this family. It was clear that the husband was a "stuck" mover and the wife had become a "stuck" opposer. Freeing these roles enabled the wife to take more initiative, and to offer more commentary from the position of a bystander. At the same time, the husband was enabled to step back from his pushy initiator position and have the perspective of a bystander, as well as to exercise, him for the first time, some of the follower role that he had never found within his family of origin.

In the follow-up interviews with the couple, it appeared to me that the theories of family therapy that had been most validated by this brief experiment had been those of Bowen. The opportunity for differentiation of the self within the family appeared to be the single most helpful thing that had happened to this couple. Both of them agreed that listening to one another and separating his own thoughts from feelings in the exercise of self-differentiation had been extremely valuable. The Bowen model, differentiating thought from feeling, was useful for its indication of techniques to apply to the therapy. The role-playing technique was an outgrowth of my awareness that each partner was so caught in and flooded by the affect between them that he was unable to think clearly about the implications of his own behavior. Back-to-back listening was another technique dictated by the Bowen model. A reduction in cues interfered with the affective overload, allowing a cognitive perspective to develop. Both agreed that the process of listening to one another in this way had been quite facilitating. Each had become more self-aware, and consequently less angry and less demanding toward the other. A greater self-awareness also contributed to an enhanced appreciation of the boundaries between self and other. An increased confidence in the integrity of personal boundaries reduced the need for distancing and pursuit behavior.

Patrick's changes led also to a shift in his family of origin, which he felt to be quite remarkable. He had been able to draw closer to his mother and end the cut-off with her, and also to make overtures toward his brother for the beginning of a relationship for the first time in their adult lives. Shaken by the discovery of his ambivalence and the ambiguity of his own feelings, Patrick was able to drop his stance of superiority. This allowed Elly to have space to be competent and articulate in her own right. He was able to describe needs and feelings of his own for the first time, rather than being stuck in the position of a conquering hero who passed on to his wife his disavowed attitudes. His wishes for warmth, comfort, love, gentleness and intimacy were in some ways a revelation to his wife, who had originally experienced him as the source of multiple demands and orders.

As a second chapter to a partially successful individual psychotherapy attempt, the couple's treatment was most enlightening to me as a therapist. I was able to see in the couple the use of the husband as an ego adjunct, which had been occurring with me in the transference without my being fully able to grasp its development and significance. The nature of the object relations became much clearer in the couple therapy than I was ever able to make them in individual therapy, and consequently more accessible to therapeutic intervention. Although post-partum depression can be successfully treated in an individual psychotherapy, seeing the symptoms in the context of a couple's dynamics permits an alteration of the system with which the individual interacts. This change in the family system can contribute to, as well as complement, intrapsychic change. It was fortuitous that the impasse in this individual psychotherapy led us into a different mode. The couple therapy was a most useful supplement to the individual therapy, allowing us to extend our explorations and leading to a much more satisfactory outcome.

REFERENCES

Beck, A.T. Depression. New York, Hoeber Medical Division of Harper and Row, 1967.

Bowen, M. Family therapy in clinical practice. New York, Jason Aronson, 1978.

Fogarty, T. Marital crisis. In Guerin, P. (Ed.). Family therapy. New York, Gardner Press, 1976.

Frank, J.D. Persuasion and healing. New York, Shocken Books, 1974.

Friedman, L.J. Personal communication, 1977.

Kantor, J., & Lehr, W. Inside the family. San Francisco, Jossey-Bass, 1975.

Minuchin, S. Structural family therapy. Cambridge, Harvard University Press, 1974.

Sacks, J. M. The Letter. *Group Psychotherapy,* 1974, *27*, 184–190.

Watzlawick, P. Weakland, J., & Fisch, R. The gentle art of reframing. In Change: Principles of problem formation and problem resolution. New York, W. W. Norton, 1974.

Yablonsky, L. Psychodrama. New York, Basic Books, 1976.

Norman I. Moss, M.D.

4

Family Therapy with a Seriously Depressed or Psychotic Identified Patient

In this chapter I will focus on the common clinical situation where there is a seriously troubled, identified patient and the family is *not* asking for help for themselves.

When working with families it is helpful to be explicit about the purpose of family meetings. Both in negotiating a working alliance with the family and in my own conceptualization, I find it useful to separate family work into three levels of increasing complexity and commitment: (1) to aid in the evaluation of the identified patient; (2) to counsel the family with reference to the identified patient; and (3) to treat the entire family, including the identified patient. My reasons for recommending explicit categorization are:

1. Candidness in approaching a family is a requisite for building up a working alliance. Unless the family has directly requested counseling or therapy, attempts to use the intrusive techniques that family therapy requires will be shunned by the family and create an atmosphere of distrust.
2. The identified patients I will be referring to are, in fact, significantly impaired in their psychosocial functions (severely depressed, manic-depressive, schizophrenic.) It seems to me both premature, from a scientific standpoint, and tactically erroneous in terms of the family's initial assumptions, to

suggest family therapy to such families immediately. Their own assessment is that the identified patient is, in fact, very troubled. The issue of whether or not he or she is scapegoated (i.e., blamed for other family problems that do not directly result from his or her behavior), is one which is difficult to approach until the initial focus has been placed on the identified patient whose actual troubled behavior provides a magnet for projective identification of the intrapsychic and interpersonal conflicts of other family members. This sets up a rigid system that is difficult to explore or challenge without an explicit and firm contract.

3. Inviting the family in for a meeting to "aid in better understanding" the patient is usually the least threatening format for meeting the family and for beginning to assess the following complex questions: to what degree does the patient use the family to grow or regress; to what degree are various family members motivated to encourage growth; or, conversely, to what degree do they need to have the patient remain at a low level of functioning?

DIAGNOSTIC PHASE

With a cooperative family, I usually suggest an open-ended diagnostic evaluation focused on the identified patient and tell them I will make some counseling kinds of remarks during the evaluation if they wish. After three-to-six diagnostic meetings, I usually have had enough time to develop some working hypotheses about the aforementioned questions and to develop empathic bonds and a sense of trust with each family member. With this as a basis, if it is indicated, I can then recommend counseling or family therapy. In these diagnostic sessions I ask that everyone living with the patient be present and that important members of the extended family be present for at least one meeting.

Most resistance to these meetings comes from male members of the family (husbands or fathers), from paranoid family members, from the existence of a powerful family secret, and finally, from an identified patient who has been physically intimidated by a family member. In such resistant cases, I firmly underscore the importance of family meetings for the understanding and treatment of the patient, and, if necessary, I negotiate a fixed, small number of meetings. For example, if a resistant husband argues that his work prevents him from coming, or that he is not part of the problem, I suggest that we meet three times—no more, no less. The clinical setting in which these meetings take place is an important factor. On an in-patient service the clinician has leverage. On an outpatient basis, however, I suggest these family meetings only after the first meeting with the patient alone.

During this diagnostic phase, I try to assess not only the aforementioned issues of family maintenance and/or projection of psychopathology, but also to decide whether therapy would be more likely to succeed with me or with another therapist (e.g., a woman therapist or a person of the family's own ethnic background.) I try to understand the family concept of psychological causality and possibilities for psychological change. There are many intellectually sophisticated people who, either because of cultural values or underlying feelings of despair, do not believe that change in their own behavior is possible. If this is an issue, it needs to be addressed, directly and repeatedly, early in the course of the evaluation and therapy. The therapist must ask, "Do you think that a person can change his/her behavior?" Finally, the level of goodwill toward the patient and within the family unit itself must be evaluated. This is sometimes difficult to accomplish in the initial meetings. Feelings of love may be covered up by years of accumulated frustration, bitterness, and increasing hopelessness. In the absence of affection it is very difficult, if not impossible, to produce change in a family. When there is love or goodwill remaining, however, much therapeutic work can be done—in spite of significant resistance and severe psychological problems.

COUNSELING PHASE

I use the counseling model when my evaluation shows that the three following factors are *all* present:

1. when the patient, apart from any family interaction, has significant individual problems, and is either living at home, or is emotionally and financially dependent on the family (e.g., a 38-year-old paranoid schizophrenic son, responsive to Stelazine, living at home with mother, father, and unmarried sister);

2. when the family appears well-motivated to help the patient
    (this motivation could come from feelings toward the patient
    or it could come from the family's desire to minimize their
    own pain that behavior of the patient has caused);
3. when the family members do *not* appear to be neurotically
    driven to maintain the patient's maladaptive behavior.

The counseling model engenders less resistance than a recommendation for "family therapy." The therapist may, however,
in the course of counseling, reverse his or her initial evaluation of
the family members and attempt to negotiate a contract for
therapy; for example, a therapist assigns a task to a family
member, he or she fails to carry it out, exploration of the failure
reveals a neurotic component in the family's relationship with the
patient or a triangle in which the patient is involved. Clarification of this issue provides a solid platform for recommending
"therapy."

In both the diagnostic and counseling models, I ask each
family member to express their view of the problem; to state what
they would like to see changed and what they fear might result
from the meetings. If they spontaneously raise family problems
that are not dynamically related to the identified patient, I acknowledge their statement and indicate that if their view is
shared by other family members, or if they can convince the other
person that this problem does, in fact, exist, I would be willing to
work with them on the issue. I make clear, however, that the
initial focus will still be on the identified patient. The only historical material I ask for that is not about the identified patient, is a
"family history" and similar or related problems in both parents'
families of origin. If family members bring up personal history, I
initially only respond to that facet of it that directly relates to the
immediate problem. In the course of either diagnostic or counseling work with families, I may suggest to family members that
they seek individual, couple, or family therapy.

FAMILY THERAPY

Before discussing the specific issues of family therapy, I
would like to clarify that, in my practice, I view family therapy as
only one of a number of modalities of therapy. I usually will

employ it as a complement to both individual psychotherapy and pharmacotherapy.

Relative contraindications to family therapy are:

1. An acutely confused and fragmented patient or other significant family member (severe manic, markedly disorganized, acute schizophrenic).

2. No family exists in the affective-libidinal sense of the word, a family where there are neither the bonds of affection nor of hate/need. These may be families that have closed ranks and have abandoned a chronically ill member, who, in turn, has cut all affective ties to the family; or they may be markedly dispersed and uninvolved families. In the case of a motivated *individual* from this type of family (motivated either by individual needs or needs to reconstitute or rescue their families), Bowen's "coaching" techniques are very useful.

3. People in individual therapy who, at a difficult point in their therapy, are clearly "acting out" and suddenly decide that "what they really need" is couple or family therapy. I will generally see the couple or family for a brief evaluation.

Some authors, e.g., Ackerman (1966), list severe psychosomatic disease and marked paranoia as contraindications. I find that I must evaluate each case separately and often over several meetings. I have treated a few families where a member had severe ulcerative colitis or regional enteritis, and have found that I had to give that person a good deal of empathic support and let him/her pace the movement of the family therapy, especially during the initial stages.

Guttman (1973) and Beals (1976) have suggested that the first acute psychotic break in an adolescent is a contraindication to intensive conjoint family therapy. Beals' group works with the adolescent and the family separately and conclude that the adolescent needs a source other than the family in which to grow and to develop relationships.

In the diagnostic and treatment phase with families, I integrate psychodynamic and instructural concepts and techniques. A psychodynamic understanding is most useful in anticipating areas of psychological sensitivity in each family member and in choosing metaphors to speak with them about their interactions. For example, an oral hysteric mother who had recurrent severe episodes of severe depression (responsive to Tofranil), repeatedly and blatantly flirted with her two adolescent sons despite her husband's presence at the family session. I sensed her oral preoccupations, particularly in the transference, and talked with her about her concerns that there "might not be enough nurturance to go around," and that "one person might grow at the expense of the other's survival." As we addressed these anxieties, her flirtatiousness decreased and could be better understood. This had been her way of trying to maintain control of the men whom she saw as nurturing figures, and to ensure that if anyone were destroyed, it would be the men, killing one another. A psychodynamic understanding of each individual is also helpful in the selection and timing of structural task assignments and decisions to work with different family subsystems.

Awareness of the power of oedipal dynamics that operate even in these often pregenitally fixated couples warns the therapist of the specific ways in which his or her gender will influence the marital pair's response (e.g., woman therapists are usually less threatening to the dominant male or paranoid male).

A psychodynamic focus on the family as a whole can clarify: (1) the developmental stage of the family; (2) the specific developmental tasks not mastered by the parents and therefore compromising their parenting ability; and (3) any shared libidinal preoccupations or anxieties, such as, competition, dominant submissiveness, and separation anxiety.

SPECIFIC CLINICAL ISSUES COMMON TO THESE FAMILIES

Denial

Denial by the family of the seriousness and/or chronicity of the patient's illness is usually maintained by a combination of the following psychodynamic factors, each of which needs to be separately acknowledged and worked through:

1. *Neurotic guilt*—based on omnipotent fantasies and/or unacceptable feelings of hostility—that is used as a defense against feelings of helplessness.
2. *Shame*—based on narcissistic identification with the patient (i.e., there must be something sick about me if I parented/ married such a sick person.)

3. *Fear*—especially when the patient is clearly chronically ill, homicidal, or suicidal. It is important for the therapist to talk about these specific dangers in a matter-of-fact manner. With regard to the suicidal patient, it is useful to start by asking the patient a question. I ask, "Whose responsibility is it if you kill yourself?" Then, going around the room, I ask the same question to each family member. One can then sort out with the family members what they can be reasonably expected to do to minimize the risk of suicide.

With regard to homicidal risk, the same technique is useful. This risk is greatest when there is a prior history of assaultive behavior, or when there is a diagnosis of paranoid schizophrenia or a full-blown manic state, and especially if the patient also uses alcohol or amphetamines. A specific couple constellation that is most precarious is one in which one spouse fits into one of the aforementioned categories and the other is a masochistic, provocative person.

When family members resist exploring these issues, I firmly focus on the intrapsychic conflicts that lead them to feel bound to the patient, e.g., pre-oedipal dependency issues (I can't live with her and I can't live without her).

REINFORCEMENT OF PATIENT'S MALADAPTIVE BEHAVIOR

The Depressed Patient

In the case of the manic-depressive, the spouse (or parent, if the patient is still living with the family of origin) may often be a superego representative. The patient relates to the partner as a highly idealized and overvalued love object in whom all his or her love is invested. The patient is willing to sacrifice everything in the marital relationship in the hope of getting love and praise from the idealized partner. Often, just before an episode of depression or mania, the patient may stage an aborted rebellion against the spouse. In the depressive phase, the depressive self-accusations may be a mirror image of the patient's appraisal of the spouse, and may give an uncanny description of the spouse. One transactional function of the depression is an attempt to force the partner into the role of the good, nurturant parent. The partner, however, soon becomes sensitized to the sadistic attack hidden in the depressive self-accusations and somatic complaints.

The specific psychological constellations in the spouse that are challenged by the depressed patient's improvement are: the paranoid spouse (this paranoia may often be circumscribed to the marital relationship); the psychopathic spouse (gambling, illegal business dealings, extra-marital affairs, etc.); a projective identification of a depressed self or an object representation. The "healthy" spouse needs a depressed spouse to work out interpersonally what is truly either a depressed intrapsychic self or an important object representation. The recovery of the patient may often precipitate a depression in the healthy spouse. This may occur within a few weeks or after several months. These depressions, however, are usually amenable to psychotherapy.

Even if the spouse is a mature and affectionate individual, he or she is eventually pushed by the depressed person's complaints into aggressive counterattacks that intensify the patient's pathological feelings of worthlessness. Thus, a vicious cycle is set in motion.

In both the depressed and schizophrenic group, the therapist must be wary (especially in the initial few sessions) of the possibility that the identified patient will try to use these sessions as a forum to attack and humiliate those family members whom he feels have victimized him. If the patient's attacks are not checked or modified by the therapist, they can destroy any possibility of a working alliance with these family members.

The Schizophrenic Patient

The spouses and families, in my experience, cover a broad spectrum. This spectrum curves from the relatively healthy to the most symbiotic and undifferentiated. One marital dyad that requires caution on the therapist's part is that of a schizophrenic married to a rigid, compulsive partner. The schizophrenic appears to borrow the partner's compulsive reaction formations to strengthen his/her own compulsive defenses against threatening psychotic fragmentation. Sometimes this backfires: the compulsiveness of the partner may periodically become intolerably oppressive for the schizophrenic person and may precipitate a crisis.

In evaluating a family with a schizophrenic patient, it is important to ascertain, in terms of prognosis, whether the patient has *ever* made an affective and communicative bond with family members. If not, one can anticipate a long therapy while trying to create what has never existed before. If communication on a higher level has existed, and had been recently compromised by a developing psychosis, then the work is proportionately shorter and more likely to be successful.

TECHNIQUE

With regard to techniques, a major concern of dynamic psychotherapy is the wording and timing of our interventions so that they cause the minimal narcissistic wound to the patient and produce no more anxiety than the therapeutic relationship can bear. These two technical issues are especially challenging for a therapist working with families where there is often marked narcissistic vulnerability and a high anxiety level. Initially, I encourage the family to focus on the relatively low-charged emotional issue of the patient's developmental life-phase (e.g., adolescence) and how this may be related to the family's life-stage (e.g., impending "empty nest"). These developmental metaphors allow the patient and family more objectivity and a greater sense of participation in a universal human experience, rather than an arcane, pathological one. Later, I may shift to a multigenerational perspective that is more charged than the developmental stage, but that still minimizes the issues of blame and guilt and helps to frame the current crisis for both the family and the therapist. As a long-range goal, I encourage the family to work with me to identify the repeated, patterned sources of crisis, and to anticipate future crises that may result from forthcoming individual and family developmental phases.

The most tenacious issue in the family therapy of many schizophrenic patients and some severe borderlines is the family's reaction to the patient as a separate person whose very urge to grow is felt to be a threat to their own survival and sanity. This system, fear of the patient, is maintained by a combination of the following dynamics, each of which usually needs to be separately identified and resolved:

1. projection of hostile impulses and/or disowned craziness onto the schizophrenic patient,

2. shared oral fixations;
3. shared belief that hostile impulses and thoughts are destruc-
    tive (for example, a hostile thought or feeling, some families
    believe, will concretely harm another person and will result
    in retaliation; this makes tolerance of ambivalence very dif-
    ficult);
4. symbiotic situations where there is no model of healthy re-
    latedness and where relationships are seen either as symbio-
    tic or as agonizing states of unrelatedness and/or a mutual
    death and the therapist must suggest alternate models;
5. families where the child as a "delegate," bound by either fear
    of annihilation and/or loyalty to do a parent's mission, must
    prove parent's anxious overprotectedness is warranted, de-
    stroy one parent out of loyalty to the other, or prove parent's
    projected "craziness" is valid (Boszormeny-Nagy; Spark,
    1973; Stierlin, 1977).

   Finally, it is important to have all children in the family
present, at least in the diagnostic phase, with play material
available, while the therapist pays attention to the effect the
serious psychological problems of the parent is having on the
development of the child.

BIBLIOGRAPHY

Ackerman, N. Treating the troubled family. New York, Basic Books,
    1966.
Ackerman, N. Child Participation in Family Therapy. *Family Process.*
    1970, *4,* 403–410.
Anthony, E.J. The Mutative Impact on Family Life of a Serious Mental
    Illness or Physical Illness of a Parent. *Canadian Psychiatric Associa-
    tion Journal.* 1969, *14,* 433–453.
Beck, A.T. Depression: Causes and treatment. University of Pennsyl-
    vania Press, 1967.
Beals, C.C. *In* Guerin, P. (Ed.). Family therapy: Theory and practice.
    New York, Gardner Press, 1976.
Boszormeny-Nagy, I. & Framo, J. Intensive family therapy. New York,
    Harper and Row, 1965.
Boszormeny-Nagy, I. & Spark, G.M. Invisible loyalties. Hagerstown,
    Md., Harper & Row, 1973.

Guttman, H. A Contraindication for Family Therapy. *Archives of General Psychiatry.* 1973, *29,* 352–355.

Jacobson, E. Depression. New York, International University Press, 1971.

Lesse, S. Apparent Remissions in Depressed Suicidal Patients. *The Journal of Nervous and Mental Disease.* 1967, *144,* 291–296.

Lion, J., & Pasternak, S. Countertransference Reactions to Violent Patients. *American Journal of Psychiatry.* 1973, *130,* 207–210.

Maltsberger, J., & Buie, D. Countertransference Hate in the Treatment of Suicidal Patients. *Archives of General Psychiatry.* 1974, *30,* 627–633.

Mintz, R.S. Basic Considerations in the Psychotherapy of the Depressed Suicidal Patient. *American Journal of Psychotherapy.* 1971, *25,* 561–573.

Pittman, F. Managing acute psychiatric emergencies. *In* Bloch, D. (Ed.). Techniques of family therapy. New York, Grune and Stratton, 1973.

Pittman, F. Managing acute psychiatric emergencies. *In* Papp, P. (Ed.). Family therapy. New York, Gardner Press, 1977, pp. 1–22.

Searles, H. Collected papers on schizophrenia. New York, International University Press, 1965, pp. 721–751.

Shapiro, E., Edward, R., Zinner, J., & Shapiro, R.R. The Influence of Family Experience on Borderline Personality Development. *International Review of Psychoanalysis.* 1975, *2,* 399–411.

Singer, M.T., & Wynne, L.C. Thought Disorder and Family Relations of Schizophrenics. *Archives of General Psychiatry.* 1965, *12,* 187–211.

Stierlin, H. Psychoanalysis and family therapy. New York, Aronson, 1977.

Tarrier, N., Vaughn, C., Lacler, M., & Leff, J. Bodily Reactions to People and Events in Schizophrenia. *Archives of General Psychiatry.* 1979, *36,* 311–315.

Leonard J. Friedman, M.D.

5
Integrating Psychoanalytic Object-relations Understanding with Family Systems Intervention in Couples Therapy

Psychoanalysis and family-systems theory have been seen as antagonistic, to the detriment of each. I have been working for the past eight years to synthesize these two different approaches in theory and practice (Friedman, 1975; 1977). I believe they are ultimately complementary, analogous to the relationship of the wave and particle theories of light. Psychoanalysis leads to a detailed understanding of meanings, providing personal psychohistorical depth while slighting the effects of on-going relational processes in problem maintenance. Only that which can be verbalized is accessible. Pure family-systems work clarifies interpersonal transactions rapidly, gaining breadth while losing depth. Integrating these two powerful approaches uses the strength of both to facilitate problem resolution.

Object-relations thinking in Freudian psychoanalysis began with the work of Klein (1948), but was principally developed by Fairbairn (1952), Balint (1952), Winnicott (1965; 1971), Dicks (1967), and Guntrip (1961) in England. Sullivan (1956) was an important early contributor to a psychology of interpersonal relationships among the neo-Freudians. This area of psychoanalysis is the current growing region. It finds dynamic and personal historical reasons for problems in current relationships.

Family-systems thinking began in the United States in the

late 50s, with the work of Ackerman (1958; 1966), Bowen (1976), Lidz (1963), Whitaker (Napier, 1978), Bateson (1972), Jackson & Weakland (1961), Haley (1976), and others. This position has been expanded by Minuchin (1974), Boszormenyi-Nagy & Spark (1973), Satir (Bandler, et al., 1976; Satir, 1974), Kantor & Lehr (1975), Framo (1965), Slipp (1976), and others. It focuses on current behavior in the family, overt and covert communication processes, feedback loops, and roles. New conceptual language had to be developed to encompass social-psychological events, creating a new paradigm.

Reducing object-relations theory to its central thesis, this phase of psychoanalytic theory asserts that early childhood relationships, especially those with a person's parents, shape adult relationships with respect to wishes, expectations, and fears. From this base, it is a small step further to view a person's map, or model of relationships, at the action level, as arising by generalizations from early family experiences with all family members, including siblings (Toman, 1969), grandparents, uncles, aunts, and cousins, including what is imagined and distorted.

Mapping is a bridging concept that I will develop. Specific aspects of the enormous range of human potential for feeling-behaving-believing are selectively enhanced or stunted by the particular events in each family, including its heritage of values, loyalties, family wisdom and family secrets, and especially by the particular way experience is punctuated—that is, the way the flow of experience is bundled into meaningful sequences (Scheflen, 1978). This includes implications about causation, appropriateness, and expectation of specific feelings, responses, or convictions under particular circumstances; and the degree to which verbal messages are emphasized compared to the nonverbal channels, such as tone of voice, direction and manner of gaze, eye expressions, facial expressions, gestures, posture, or other bodily language. From all of this, as each person grows, he/she develops a model of the personally significant aspects of human experience, including representations of self and other people that becomes a map of inter- and intra-personal reality. It is somewhat different for everyone. I believe that mapping is primarily a non-dominant hemisphere function, later overlaid with verbal process, and suppressed to varying degrees.

The study by neurophysiologists of the localization of mental functions in the cerebral cortex has indicated that the left and right hemispheres serve different functions (Bogen, 1973). Which hemisphere is dominant depends on whether a person is right or left handed—it's the opposite side from the dominant hand and eye. The dominant hemisphere handles language function. A stroke there leaves a person unable to speak or understand words properly. The nondominant hemisphere is the domain of information processing and storage in a nonverbal, analog mode. What is stored is the sensory image (it can be tactile, auditory, visual, emotional) or pattern of an event. These can be recombined without words, as in dreams and creative imagination. Verbal processing is the work of the dominant hemisphere. Image-analog processing is the way the nondominant hemisphere works. Even if it turns out that these functions are not absolutely separate, referring to them as the mode of the dominant or the nondominant hemisphere is a convenient set of referents to two different modes (Watzlawick, 1978).

Under ordinary conditions there is sufficient overlap of the models used by different people for many kinds of communication to take place. This is the realm of ethnic, cultural, and personal differences, including the specific microculture of a particular family.

This mapping or model-building process continues throughout life, and is especially active during stress and during play, when a more optimum balance between surprise and familiarity can be maintained. The basic process begins when nonverbal pattern-recognition processes, localized in the nondominant cerebral hemisphere in adult life, are all the child has. Although this is later overlaid with verbal patterns, people vary in their reliance on the one and the other mode (when they conflict) under different conditions. Model construction is a way of navigating in complex environments; it provides protection against information overload, criteria of relevancy, and functions to guide attention. It supplies meanings that allow rapid orientation and response by reducing the novel to.the familiar, a lattice structure on which to attach new learning. The model grows as a crystal grows, organizing and limiting what can be learned.

I am using cognitive terminology here, but I do not wish to be misunderstood as excluding the patterns of feeling and behav-

ioral sequences that may be completely unrecognized, or unconscious. Unconsciousness need not be a matter of repression. Many
feeling-action processes are selectively attended or inattended to.
Some have no names, or must not be noticed or remarked on.
Some are simply not on the map of the known world.

Our understanding of patterns of behavior results from our
intuitive sense of what makes for a meaningful sequence. People
learn the sequences that are recurrent in their families as they
grow up. They also learn to verbalize about some, but not all, of
their behavior. Their cognitive map of the given world and what
they can expect from themselves and other people is shaped by
family experiences. Some of these expectations are held unconsciously, but with such strength that they restrict a person in his
or her interpersonal sphere. These beliefs may be compared to the
belief that the earth was flat that existed at the time of Columbus. It was only by risking sailing over the edge of the world and
finding that there was no edge that Columbus could challenge
this belief. One of the ways that a therapist helps is by serving as
a guide to experimentation in living. Restructuring belief involves small experiences that may be compared to "sailing over
the edge of the world." Treating the action mode as meaningful
allows understanding of the family system as it constitutes the
field and context in which the individual develops, i.e., in which
affective sequences, notions of what constitutes explanation, and
expectations of relationships emerge.

In this respect, it is important to consider the balance between novelty and familiarity. Pattern formation, the reduction
of the novel to the familiar, allows smooth, practised, and au-
tomatic (unconscious) processes to come into play. Novelty requires attention; it is stimulating to learning and appeals to
curiosity. Beyond an optimum, stimulus overload takes place and
anxiety develops. People vary in their appetite for the security of
familiarity (whose far border is boredom) and their pleasure in
novelty.

Play depends on an optimum balance between familiar and
novel elements, whether it be the serious plays we call art and
culture, the exciting interplay of love-making, or the relaxing
play of a familiar game. Discovery occurs in play, skills begin in
play, and we do our best analytic work when our responsiveness
has some of that quality of readiness to play together: expanding

images, responding to role inductions, being moved by the patient's experience. Play requires entering a larger system, and it is this that gives discourse its capacity to delight, stimulate, and inspire. Creativity is a high form of play.

The use of psychodramatic techniques in therapy allows immediate access to the nonverbal, affective-action sequences recorded in the nondominant hemisphere map, that are then accessible for revision. This is analogous to the way children play things out.

Originally, psychoanalysis overvalued insight learning in an effort to find a role for the conscious subjective decision within a mechanistic view of the mind that considered consciousness almost epiphenomenal. Sometimes insight precedes change. More often it accompanies it or follows it, representing the revised account of one's self that a shift in doing permits—from a new place, one can see the old more clearly. Current practice cannot ignore the learning that takes place through modeling (partial identification), trial and error, and reinforcement.

The pattern of action, particularly with obsessive problems, needs attention, lest the emphasis on knowing (through insight) and the image of the analyst Who Knows inadvertently reinforce the obsessive style or become indistinguishably isomorphic with it. It is much easier for an obsessive person to understand his psychodynamics than to risk spontaneity and affective expressiveness.

Therapy from this perspective relies on empathy to sense the patient's model of the human world; the therapist in the initial phase using his skills as explorer, map-maker, anthropologist, and pattern-detector, and checking this out from time to time with the patient. As the therapist senses the shapes of the process models in the patient's relational world, he has various options for constructive response. Highlighting the particular concordances, discrepancies, and omissions in the respective models of each of the partners is generally useful, as is relating them to particular sets of family constellations and experiences. From this arises a sense of what has no words or where words become unreliably abstract, at the edge of the known world. Discovery occurs when the therapist can dream up a move that, in a climate of safety and trust established by his empathic recognitions, encourages the patient to sail over the edge of his known world.

Effective therapy in this mode requires both the empathic skills that can lead to interpretation, if that is what is needed, and the ability to respond with a spirit of serious play that allows the therapist to join the dance and introduce variations, moving as needed into a role more like a psychodrama director or auxiliary ego. This is a different stance from that which facilitates transference development. It is a further elaboration of participant observation in an action context. The therapist's total experience informs his collaborative improvisations with his patients, the couple. This blends communicational clarification with systems interventions and interpretations that make the model of personal reality visible and palpable, along with the enactment of new sequences that can be practiced, generating and fostering hope, as the frozen inner sea melts and movement past the impasse takes place.

PRACTICAL APPLICATIONS

What do I do when I encounter a couple for the first time? It is usually a telephone call to make an appointment. I try to keep the conversation short, under 5 minutes, and focused on arranging a mutually convenient time, recording names, address, and phone numbers, with the briefest description of the problem, saying I want both partners present for that. This telephone conversation is generally enough to allow some good guesses about whether either partner is psychotic, who is more resistant to coming in, and often hints emerge about the level of despair, helplessness, hope, or anger in the partner I am speaking with. If at all possible, and it generally is, I set up a two-hour block of time for the initial appointment. My experience is that it takes that long to allow people to get past their prepared positions, to convey much of what I need to assess the state of the union, to work with the issues some, to experience some meaningful emotional relatedness to me, and to gain some grasp of what we will be doing together if we agree to continue to work.

I generally start off by remarking that they both come with various hopes and other feelings about what they would like to change about their relationship and I would like to hear about that from each of them. I am interested in who begins and how this decision is apparently reached. As I listen to the account, my style of listening is conversational, offering the kind of responsive comment that fosters the couples' sense that they are in a setting which is safe to expand into, that their expressions of feeling will be met with understanding and their fears will be respected; that they are with a person who is able to set limits, if needed, on their hurting of one another without total condemnation; a person who has had enough experience with the pleasure and pain of life, love and loss, accomplishment and disappointment, differences, imperfection, and uneven growth to recognize *them,* to meet them with compassion and humor, to challenge some of their assumptions and preoccupations, while offering a few surprises. We all have different ways of conveying this.

I want to evoke a climate for responsive interchange based on spontaneity, shaped by professional caring and awareness. As I am participating, I facilitate the unfolding of each partner's experience of the relationship, of themselves, of each other, their hopes and fears for the future. I am also getting some experience of each person's communicational style with me and with each other, the level and range of affective intensity of various sorts, including each person's sexuality, their available negotiating skills, and whether a negotiating climate exists between them. I get some ideas about the stage of personal life development each person is in and the asymmetries or congruences. I try to get a reading of the intensity and level of bonding between them, and where they are with respect to collaboration, cooperation, unrelatedness, or mutual thwarting in the life experience they are conveying. I form some impressions of how direct each can be about his/her own desires and goals, how each of them is trying to attain them, and with what results. I am interested in the degree of congruence of verbal and nonverbal messages and each person's ability to assess what he/she and the spouse offers.

At a convenient point, when each has conveyed something about the present, I shift to some bridging questions about the family of origin. Sometimes I make guesses about family constellations or elements of family style or values or affective climate, to check out the model that is growing in my own mind, to suggest that the present grows from the past without being determined by it, to convey what I am thinking and that I'm not always right. I blend questions with comments, linking one set of experiences with another, either within the person's own life or with the spouse's or my own life, and the link may be one of similarity or contrast. As we go on, I assess each person's congruence or dissonance with his/her own and the spouses' family-of-origin style, values, and images. I question how willing each is to try new things. I am sensitive to indications of a family projection process and the shape it takes, and whether there have been attempts at emotional cutoff of any family members, or other people or pursuits. I ask myself, and sometimes each of them directly, to what degree they suffer from envy, and of whom, or jealousy in some triangle.

What is the degree of depression, emotional constriction, restricting anxiety, and effective, nonantagonistic assertiveness? In what respect can each empathize with the other and how well differentiated from each other are they? How close to the limit of their frustration tolerance are each of them about crucial issues? To what extent can each accept the quid pro quo of relationship versus regressive longings, pursued through depressive or blaming efforts at control, intimidation, or extortion? It is important to get a sense of the level of separation anxiety of each, and what they value in each other.

I focus on any recurrent, frustrating patterns of affective action sequences and try to slow them down by interposing myself in some way. I use the term *snarl* for such a recurrent pattern, because it is evocative both of the intended meaning of a confused, complicated, or tangled situation and more poetically resonates with its other meaning of an angry, threatening growl, while vaguely suggesting the word *snare*—something in which they are both caught—altogether the way a snarl feels.

I get a sense of each person's realism about therapy, and how I might help and what I can't do. I am interested in the extent to which each needs what he/she dislikes and in how they trigger the worst in each other. I notice the areas in which they can present their story as a team, how they decide who will tell which parts, how and when they interrupt or contradict each other, and how this is received and responded to by the partner. I am very interested in the extent to which each can distinguish responsibility from blame or guilt. I especially note the preferred modes each person uses in structuring explanation, whether he/she has a model of causality as linear, circular, intrapersonal, interpersonal, cultural, or multilevel. Some people tend to explain their own behavior as expressing some inner state, while seeing the other person as responding. Some see the other person as expressing a feeling or motive or need, and themselves as responding or reacting.

As the process develops, I notice each person's flexibility. Accepting professional help requires some openness toward being guided and influenced toward change, some willingness to accept and try out suggestions. To what extent is this willingness present, or am I seeing a help-rejecting complainer or a person stuck in a mixture of vindictive querulousness and hateful clinging?

It is important to see each spouse alone early in therapy to find out if either one is engaged in an affair, and, if so, whether it is one whose main function is to stabilize the marriage in its unsatisfying state or whether it is an exiting affair, a prelude to dissolving the marriage. It is also an opportunity to learn about anything else the spouse has been keeping secret from the partner. I explore the person's reservations about sharing the secret with the partner, and undertake to keep the secret if the person wishes me to, making clear if I believe that keeping the secret will prevent constructive work on the marriage. Often the person with the secret reveals it directly or indirectly to the spouse before long. The meaning of this to the spouse can then be explored. If there is a rival, can the spouse compete effectively, or is the spouse paralyzed with jealous rage, righteous indignation, or feelings of self-blame or worthlessness? There is always the risk that the sense of betrayal will be fatal to the marriage, but if the basic relationship is sound, trust can often be rebuilt in time.

I have had to present these considerations in linear fashion, but these and other pattern sensitivities are part of what I am bringing to the meeting throughout. I don't pursue information in any fixed sequence. It is artificial to separate assessment dimensions from the moves I make that affect the system I am assessing; I put it this way for clarity of exposition. Sometimes my first move to shift the system occurs within the first minutes; sometimes it comes after half an hour or more, depending on what is happening. Some of my further options for constructive action, with some indications of when I use them, are highlighted below.

Requesting changes in communicational style or of communicational mode are two classes of actions that can be modelled in role playing. Tasks can be prescribed that will generate new experiences, supplementing the verbal clarification of the implicit models of the interpersonal world: the overt acknowledgement of covert processes, the recognition of conflicting loyalties, and the reopening of unresolved mourning that the object-relations model encourages. I shall give some examples of each.

With a couple for whom inattention to aspects of each other's messages is contributing to frustration and accompanying despair or anger, I suggest that they practice an exercise in which each in turn tries to repeat back without parody, distortion, or omission the message that person just received. The sender can then offer corrections. In addition to fostering accurate listening, this often highlights the characteristic communicational snarls that arise, allowing opportunities for me to clarify the distorting elements and relate them to development events.

With a couple who get into rapidly escalating quarrels in which one operates as a blamer and the other as a computer or distractor, I suggest that they continue the quarrel in a different manner. I ask them each to express their own position, but in the partner's style.

The exercises described above are both empathy-enhancing exercises and can be introduced as such. The second one also introduces an element of cognitive dissonance that tends to slow down the process and allows greater awareness of the elements each finds frustrating or confusing in the other person's style.

With couples whose battles are characterized by wordiness and indirectness, I suggest that they try the following exercise for a few minutes: Each is allowed to utter only one word to the other when it is his/her turn, with whatever body language or nonverbal embellishment will help carry the message, and they are to take turns, one word at a time, continuing the discussion. This focuses attention on the nonverbal modes and increases emotional expressiveness.

Another kind of change in communicational mode is the use of sculpture for depicting the major snarl from each person's point of view (Duhl, et al., 1973). I ask them each in turn to dream up an enactment of the impasse as each experiences it by acting as if my office is any room in their home the scene-setter wishes, and arranging the partner and then one's self in a scene that is a still-life rendition of the way it feels. One wife posed her husband in a chair in the living room, back to her, watching television, ignoring her as she talked with him. His scene had him on his back on the floor using his arms to guard his face as if from blows while he posed his wife standing at his feet, hands balled into fists on her hips, blaming him. This helped convey vividly his fear of her anger, his passive view of himself and attacking image of her, and, from her perspective, his withdrawal and ignoring of her as a passive-aggressive stance that she could not tolerate. His stance was reminiscent to her of her distant, fundamentalist father, triggering her feelings of rejection, depression, and finally anger in relation to him, as an ineffective way of making contact. Her stance, as he experienced it, reminded him of his blaming mother, whose love he tried to win by placating her and whom he distanced. One use of sculpture is to point up the different ways they experience each other, in a vivid metaphor. Another use is to simplify and dramatize the links with past experience in the family of origin.

Once the tableau has been constructed, other uses are possible. Each can be asked to set up another tableau representing a desired state of relatedness, for contrast and to objectify what is wished for. From the sculptured depiction of the snarl, the partner of the scene-setter can be asked if the position in which he/she has been placed is comfortable, and if not, to reposition in a way that is more comfortable. The same instructions are then given to the scene-setter in response to the spouse's move, and a slow motion series of interactive steps takes place. It often becomes clear how moves which make one spouse more comfortable are distressing to the other. At this point, the therapist can suggest alternative moves.

For example, in the husband's scene, with himself on the floor and his wife over him, her first move was to drop the blaming pose, step closer, and reach out a hand to help him up. He retreated further in response. I suggested that she modify her response by stepping back first to give him more space, to which he responded by getting to his knees in a placating manner. She did not like to see him this way and turned her back on him. He then got to his feet and came around to face her, since he no longer felt confronted by a blaming pursuer. From this position, when she opened her arms he could move closer to her, feeling invited to be active in a way that did not threaten him. The shift to playing it out in pantomime set up an analog to their usual snarl that was novel, playfully framed, and allowed clarification and innovation. Once changes have been made in the analog mode, insights often develop rapidly into elements of past object relations that are being re-enacted. The ways in which the partner is being set up to be a counter player in a mutually frustrating set of sequences is revealed, and hope for change is fostered. Returning then to a more discursive format, the couple and the therapist can trace out the everyday events that correspond to each phase of the sculpture, and negotiations for change can begin.

Further work can be done with the problematic object-relations models and the interactive processes that they include by using some psychodrama techniques (Leveton, 1977; Yablonsky, 1976). When some sequence of difficulty can be recognized that was elaborated in relation to a particular set of events in the family of origin, the person talking about the past can be invited to enact the parts of the other problematic family members, one at a time, so I can get the flavor of their style. If people stop themselves by saying they can't remember details, I ask them to create a plausible fiction, since I am after subjective experience, which is sometimes closer to poetic than scientific truth. I then play the patient in relation to the patient's version of the family figure in an improvised scene, first as the patient experienced the scene and then with some variations I suggest. We then trade roles and I play the family figure and the patient tries a few new variations. If it seems helpful, and if the scene involves more than two people, I invite the spouse to play one of the parts. This exercise often enables each of the spouses to notice some hitherto unobserved resemblances between the past and present, and allows discussion of new steps that can be taken in relating to the problematic members of the family of origin in the present, or opens up unresolved mourning for a dead family member, or enhances empathy with other family members whose lives can be seen in altered perspective. This work should only be attempted by experienced therapists who have had personal experience in psychodrama workshops. Because intense emotions can be released, it is important to have enough time available to allow for integration of what has been experienced before the session ends. These methods are very effective for vividly and rapidly conveying aspects of the object-relations models the patient is using.

A variety of tasks can be prescribed that will generate new experiences. One task that helps point up unrecognized identifications with parents that are complicating the couples' marriage is to ask each separately to imagine in detail what the marriage might have been like between his father and her mother, and his mother and her father. Each is to consider the strengths, difficulties, and course of each of those fictional pairings, and to write from a paragraph to a page about each before our next meeting, without discussing the task with the spouse, and to bring the homework to the next meeting, at which we will discuss it. In favorable cases, some consensus will be reached after discussion of what each imagines about those two created marriages. One of the pairings is likely to represent, in more extreme form, many of the snarls the couple is in, while the other pairing has more of their harmonious experiences or suggests shifts which would be more satisfying. If both spouses agree that both of the imagined pairings would have been disastrous, this is often a predictor of the couple themselves divorcing.

With highly enmeshed couples, I find Murray Bowen's (1976) techniques useful. With highly disengaged and affectively remote couples, I sometimes use some of George Bach's (Bach and Wyden, 1968) training exercises in constructive marital fighting. Prescriptions for homework tasks can be invented that tend to modify crucial sequences in the characteristic snarls the couple creates. For example,

Mr. A came from an enmeshed family in which differences often led to an open and continuing angry argument about who was right and what should be or should have been done. The argument went on until consensus through persuasion or guilt-induced intimidation had been reached. Interrupting the argument for a cooling off period and reconsideration of one's position was not part of the model. Mrs. A came from a paternal authoritarian family with a mother who was the submissive follower, expressing her opposition indirectly, and in which disengagement at a point of conflict was the expected practice.

Mr. A experienced her withdrawal from conflict entirely as an effort to punish him with dreaded separation, and pursued her. She experienced his desperate need to reach agreement through argument as overwhelmingly invasive, as her father was when he got drunk. Initially, she was depressed and he was helpful, but verbally explosive, when challenged.

My first homework assignment was for him to be helpful to his wife in a new way: to spend half-an-hour a day teaching her the self-assertion he excelled at, while she practiced expressing herself using her father's angry voice. This and desipramine helped her out of her depression and produced a climate more like his family, which then made him symptomatically anxious.

The next phase of the homework task involved suggesting that when an angry struggle was beginning to escalate, Mrs. A could say that she wanted to postpone further discussion of the matter for a definite length of time, up to 24 hours, the couple to agree on a time when discussion would resume in a calmer atmosphere. He could accept this as an improvement after he established that her style was to cool off during the interval and that she was not indeed angrily brooding over schemes to punish him, and his anxiety cleared up. Both learned new negotiating skills and new modes of expression, and were able to revise some aspects of their respective models of marriage.

Here are a few common problematic pairings with their associated snarls. A man who hides his separation fears and unresolved denied dependency needs under a cloak of the culturally supported traditional male image—unemotional, independent, highly self-controlled, an effective problem solver—finds a woman whose dependency is right up front, someone for whom nothing goes quite right, eager for help, whom he can take care of. Soon she begins to feel dominated and unloved, and he starts to feel dominated and exploited. From this position there are further variations depending on how each deals with anger. If he is explosive and she is placating, or if she is explosive and he is placating, one kind of snarl develops. If one is a distancer and the other is a pursuer, another kind of snarl develops. In either case, what she used to admire as reliability in him, she now calls rigidity. What he used to admire as spontaneity in her, he now views as randomness. The compulsive self-doubter and the righteous blamer have a way of finding one another and reinforcing that aspect of each other by their complementarity.

Another pattern of difficulty is the rescuer/victim/persecutor rondo. I call it a rondo because the parts turn out to be cyclically repetitive. One example is the young couple who find each other remarkably understanding and supportive of the difficulties each is having with one or both parents, who are experienced as depriving, unloving, or cruel. The implicit hope is that each will be the desired perfect parent to the other. With the advent of the first or second child, if not sooner, this breaks down; one or both feels unsupported and misunderstood and attributes the bad parent image to the other, sometimes turning the originally "bad" parent or some other person into the rescuer, sometimes seeing the child as victim of the spouse and in need of rescuing. Without time to elaborate, I want to say that I often include one or more children in the therapy for a session or two, and the parents of each when a convenient time arises, or sometimes a sibling, with the invitation being to help in the work by giving me their perspective on things. Children take naturally to the techniques of enacting events, and it is particularly illuminating with those 7-to-14-years old who are relatively monosyllabic in their style with a stranger.

To balance the perspective, I want to tell you that most of the time I am working with couples, we are sitting in chairs discussing their problems. I have focused my discussion on interactional techniques that, in practice, are integrated with my psychodynamic developmental perspective, because this is the growing edge of my current work. I have talked of patterns and abstracted elements from live experience, and before closing, I want to correct the impression of stereotyping that doing so creates.

I am fascinated with the many variations of the intense pair bonding that occurs when people form couples, and have learned to refrain from imposing any ideal image of mental health on the couple. I am repeatedly impressed with the creative possibilities that a couple can open up if the relationship is basically sound. I want to compare the kaleidoscopic richness of family process with dancing, with all of the dances elaborated by people in all cultures and epochs, some more formalized, some more predictable, but ever new. Patterns emerge but are never the same. This is the process world of Heraclitus, in which we cannot step twice in the same river, not the world of stable Platonic essences in which the knower is split from the known.

BIBLIOGRAPHY

Ackerman, N. The psychodynamics of family life. New York, Basic Books, 1958.

Ackerman, N. Treating the troubled family. New York, Basic Books, 1966.

Bach, G.R., & Wyden, P. The intimate enemy. New York, Avon Books, 1968.

Balint, M. Primary love and psychoanalytic technique. London, Hogarth Press, 1952.

Bandler, R., Grinder, J., & Satir, V. Changing with families. Palo Alto, California, Science and Behavior Books, 1976.

Bateson, G. Steps to an ecology of mind. New York, Ballantine Books, 1972.

Bogen, J.E. The Other Side of the Brain: An Appositional Mind. *Bulletin of the Los Angeles Neurological Societies,* 1969, *34,* 135–162. reprinted in Ornstein, R.E. (Ed.), The Nature of human consciousness. San Francisco, W.H. Freeman and Company, 1973.

Boszormenyi-Nagy, I., & Spark, G.M. Invisible loyalties. Hagerstown, Md., Harper & Row, 1973.

Bowen, M. Theory in the practice of psychotherapy. *In* Guerin, P.J. (Ed.). Family therapy. New York, Gardner Press, 1976.

Dicks, H.V. Marital tensions. New York, Basic Books, 1967.

Duhl, F.J., Kantor, D., & Duhl, B.S. Learning, space, and action in family therapy: A primer of sculpture. *In* Bloch, D.A. (Ed.). Techniques of family psychotherapy. New York, Grune and Stratton, 1973.

Fairbairn, W.R.D. Psychoanalytic studies of the personality. London, Tavistock Publications Limited, 1952.

Framo, J.L. Rationale and techniques of intensive family therapy. *In* Boszormenyi-Nagy, I., & Framo, J.L. (Eds.). Intensive family therapy. New York, Harper and Row, 1965.

Friedman, L.J. Current Psychoanalytic Object Relations Theory and Its Clinical Implications. *International Journal of Psycho-Analysis.* 1975, *56,* 137–146.

Friedman, L.J. Object relations in psychoanalytic technique. In *International encyclopedia of psychiatry, psychology, psychoanalysis, and neurology.* New York, Aesculapius Publishers, 1977.

Guntrip, H. Personality structure and human interaction. New York, International Universitites Press, 1961.

Haley, J. Problem-solving therapy. San Francisco, Jossey-Bass, 1976.

Jackson, D.D., and Weakland, J.H. Conjoint Family Therapy: Some Considerations on Theory, Technique and Results. *Psychiatry,* 1961, *24,* 30–45.

Kantor, D., & Lehr, W. Inside the family. San Francisco, Jossey-Bass, 1975.

Klein, M. Contributions to psychoanalysis 1921–1945. London, Hogarth Press, and the Institute of Psychoanalysis, 1948.

Leveton, E. Psychodrama for the timid clinician. New York, Springer Publishing Company, 1977.

Lidz, T. The family and human adaptation. New York, International Universities Press, 1963.

Minuchin, S. Families and family therapy. Cambridge, Harvard University Press, 1974.

Napier, A.Y., with Whitaker, C.A. The family crucible. New York: Harper and Row, 1978.

Satir, V. Conjoint family therapy. Palo Alto, California, Science and Behavior Books, 1964.

Scheflen, A.E. Susan Smiled: On Explanation in Family Therapy. *Family Process.* 1978, *17,* 59–68.

Slipp, S. An Intrapsychic-Interpersonal Theory of Depression. *Journal of the American Academy of Psychoanalysis.* 1976, *4,* 389–409.

Sullivan, H.S. Clinical studies in psychiatry. New York, W.W. Norton & Company, 1956.

Toman, W. Family constellation (2nd ed.). New York, Springer Publishing Company, 1969.

Watzlawick, P. The language of change. New York, Basic Books, 1978.

Winnicott, D.W. The maturational processes and the facilitating environment. New York, International Universities Press, 1965.

Winnicott, D.W. Playing and reality. New York, Basic Books, 1971.

Yablonsky, L. Psychodrama. New York, Basic Books, 1976.

Kitty La Perriere, Ph.D.

6
On Children, Adults, and Families: The Critical Transition From Couple to Parents

Ten or twelve years ago, I had an appointment to see a young couple for an evaluation for family therapy. They had one eighteen-month-old daughter, and the mother was pregnant again. The presenting symptom, the mother's depression, was so severe that she spent days in bed unable to move. Individual therapy had been tried. She had refused to speak to the therapist and was diagnosed as borderline. The family arrived for their first appointment on the day of the Institute Christmas party. On the way from the waiting room to my office, we passed the room where some mild festivities were going on and joined them briefly. Mother and father each took a drink, and the little girl asked for and received a glass, asked for and received ice cubes, and with help, sat in an adult chair and pretended to sip a drink. Both parents proudly smiled at the precocity of their daughter, and I joined them in their admiration. Later on, in my office, I noticed that the little girl was remarkably self-contained. Again she sat in her own chair and played with a toy. I began to wonder, however, about her mature behavior. Somewhere toward the end of the session, the little girl inclined her head and put her thumb in her mouth. Father said, "You are tired," and mother said, "You know what to do," whereupon the child went to a bag, pulled out a blanket, cuddled it to her face, and closed her eyes. It was while I

81

observed that my perception of the situation changed: what had in the beginning seemed like remarkable self-reliance and re-sourcefulness in the child suddenly acquired a dimension of sad-ness and deprivation. I had subtly shifted my frame-of-reference and slipped from an adult world into a child-centered world.

ON MOTHER-INFANT OBSERVATION

Prior to this experience, I had spent a number of years ob-serving mother-child pairs in a developmental study headed by Dr. Margaret Mahler. The experience of the Mahler (1978) study was with me as I studied the child in my office. Un-dertaken by Dr. Mahler to get normative data on normal child-hood development, the study was undertaken to obtain a com-parison base for the deviant development of autistic children. The study acquired a much more general importance, however, be-cause of the close observation of the process by which an infant becomes a person, and because of the kinds of data that were collected. We observed a small number of mother—child pairs for several hours a week over a period of two-to-three years. Mothers would bring their children to the Center, where a special room was set up. This room was adapted to the children's comfort and staffed with participant-observers who acted as companions and facilitators to the mothers and children. But although we ob-served mother and infant in interaction, and thus thought of our study as, in effect, an interpersonal one, the whole format of the study was child-centered. The entire setting was addressed to the needs of the infant, and to the needs of the mothers only as the caretakers of the infants. Now, as I work with the problem mothers face in families, I understand, in retrospect, the kind of protected slice-of-life represented by our observation of the mother-infant interaction in the Center. The mothers were in a refuge from their usual world. The resources and the sociability of the Center, the interest of other adults in the children, the relief from cleaning up, the help with child care—all of these things made the mother's situation a very special one. We were observ-ing infants only; the mothers were simply the hands and eyes and arms required by the infant. I don't think that we attempted at any time to seriously relate what was going on in that room to what was going on in the rest of the mother's life. Even though occasional home visits were made to the families of the children, our outlook was always child-centered. We focused on the child, and everyone else became relevant only in their function vis-à-vis the child.

As I sat in the room and observed the little girl's behavior, the set of comparison data from the infant-observation study began to affect my thoughts as a family therapist. I began to wonder whether this child, in addition to being hypermature, self-contained, and resourceful, might also be undernurtured, undercomforted, and prematurely self-reliant. These kinds of questions, even as I raise them now, still do not seem incompatible to me. I want to stress that experience, thoughts, and formulations coming from different universes of study and endeavor, sometimes combine to create unusual insights. In this particular situation, I was able to raise the question of dependency, of gratification of need, of the entitlement to support and sustenance, into a central family theme. Seeing parents training their child so that "she would not have the same problems we are having," helped address important issues in the first session and provided a good start for therapy. The details of the therapy are not relevant to this chapter; let me just say that the mother got better, the marriage improved, the parents learned more relaxed parenting, and went on to have two more children whom they parented joyfully and competently. Perhaps my sensitivity to the issues of infancy had helped, or perhaps my enthusiasm as a beginning therapist did. Whatever the reasons, the good outcome of that experience helped make me particularly interested in working with families with small children.

I have noticed that family therapists are often reluctant to have children who are below rational speaking age attend family sessions. It has been my experience that seeing parents, at least in the diagnostic meetings, but preferably in later sessions as well, with all their children present, gives important information to the therapist about the way in which essential basic human needs are handled by the family. For example: who takes care of the child; who holds the child; how much eye contact exists between infant and parent; what kind of safety precautions are taken; what is the anxiety and care level the parents direct toward each of their children; and which of the parents does the parenting and when. We often overlook these questions while observing families from an adult point of view.

Division between Child and Adult World in the Mental Health Professions

Specializations in the mental health profession fall along age lines and separate the child-centered point of view from the adult-centered point of view. Very little information crosses the boundary line, and what does gets distorted in the crossing. Professional practices and educational curricula are built as though one could understand, describe, and deal with children without taking into account their parents and their surroundings. In adult-to-adult talk, the experience of, and with, children is often neglected.

The student entering the mental health world has to choose. She either learns a lot about children or she learns a lot about adults. Professionals become indoctrinated into one or the other point of view. Pediatricians, child therapists, or teachers often become adult fearers and adult haters; they side with the children against unfeeling, incompetent, selfish, and uncaring parents. Adult therapists often forget the conditions and requirements of childhood, and their conceptualizations allow little space for the child's realities. Sometimes this conflict is played out among therapists. A scenario that used to be familiar in child guidance settings was one in which the child's therapist, caught up in being a better parent, began to compete with and hate the child's actual parents. The parents' therapist, meanwhile, joined the parents in scapegoating the child and felt sorry for their misfortune.

In addition to educators and clinicians, researchers also honor this split. We forget that our observational methodology determines what we see. The child who is studied in isolation appears to be totally governed by an inner clock that times his/ her growth and unfolding. Most normative studies of infant development use this approach. They study affect, reactivity, intelligence, and motor skills, without noting the interpersonal and social context of the process.

The mother-child observation tradition is one step removed from viewing the child in isolation. It is, however, still a methodology that does not take into account the embeddedness of this dyad in the larger family structure. It does not reflect the role and participation of father, of siblings, of grandparental generations; nor does it take into account any of the larger, social class, cultural, and ethnic variations.

In the adult-centered world, we sometimes give people paper and pencil questionnaires that ask about their attitudes toward children and child-rearing practices. We do elaborate research based on the results of these questionnaires as though they reflected very much of the actual living events between parents and children.

Family therapy, on the other hand, knows relatively little about the basic issues between parents and children, at least those of early infancy and childhood. Much of the family-therapy world-view is derived from office visits and language; children are often excluded until they are old enough to behave through a session and to participate in adult-like transactions. Family-therapy training does not emphasize child development findings, and not many family therapists are acquainted with them. Some family therapists dispense with seeing children altogether, and work only with and through the adults, who are seen as the main power holders and definers of family functioning. Those aspects of the adult that relate to issues of early childhood do not make an appearance in the world of family therapy.

Separateness of the Adult World from the World of Children

The separation of children and adults in the professional mental health world corresponds to the reality of the social organization of our everyday world at large. The public, adult world of work, of politics, and even of literature and science does not concern itself much with the needs of children and parents. The requirements and the anxieties that go with looking after small children are seldom acknowledged and even more rarely attended to usefully. The presence of small children becomes a factor that usually serves to exclude the care-taking parent, most often the mother, from responsible employment. Even though, according to recent statistics, over 50 percent of women above the age of sixteen are in the active labor force, provisions for help with child care hardly exist. In addition, most health insurance plans do not even include benefits for the cost of normal pregnancy.

The child-care functions receive little social support. Until recently, expenses for child care could not be deducted from income tax, and can be deducted now only to a very limited extent. Baby sitters are among the least qualified help in existence. Usually totally untrained, these sitters are often barely screened, and poorly paid. Their relationship to the family is nebulous, and at times they are merely strangers sent by an agency. There are no guidelines by which to evaluate their competence, and no methods of testing their values and attitudes for compatibility with those of the family. These difficulties may be more pronounced in large cities. There are, of course, many satisfactory baby sitting arrangements made; for example, in small towns where babysitting is done by the neighbor's children. I am not addressing those. I am commenting on how few regulations and skills do exist that pertain to the important job of looking after small children.

The existence of regulations, whether we like it or not, says much about which things we consider important. Regulations have not been created which are concerned with the child-care problem. That help with child care is not easily found, that it is not deemed important, and that no provisions are made for its availability are only part of the story. The whole affective experience of early parenthood is somehow not put into words, and does not become public domain. It is not acknowledged, not explored, not validated. The anxieties, the fatigue, and the feelings of entrapment are usually kept silent. The parents who experience them often feel that they are particularly incompetent, particularly guilty, particularly bad. It has become a trite truth that children hate their parents. The strength with which most parents sometimes hate their children remains a well kept secret. Occasionally, some dramatic story of child abuse arouses the adult world. The surprise, outrage, and incomprehension with which such events are greeted attest to the fact that some taboo against acknowledging such common experiences has been breached.

Parenting is regarded as a lower order of activity. It is not an acceptable priority in our work life, business life, social life. A father in a family I am treating was recently describing trying to leave a business meeting on a night when it was his turn to prepare dinner. As it got to be later and later, he did not know what to do. Finally, he sneaked to a corner office phone, and, cupping his hand over mouth and receiver, whispered to his 11-year-old daughter, "Please turn the oven off." He finally extricated himself from the meeting with some other excuse. A woman, I would guess, would not have found it much easier to leave an important meeting.

I do believe, however, that the resulting stress of parenting is an experience that, until recently, was predominantly experienced by women. When many men in important positions begin to leave the office to go home and prepare dinner, something will have to change—either the scheduling rules of meetings, the availability of help, or the structure of meals. Perhaps the experience of child-rearing will then be discussed publicly, the disadvantages described in detail, and the problems taken into account, and resources found to search for solutions.

THE TRANSITION FROM COUPLE TO PARENTS

The Change in Social Context

The arrival of the first child marks one of the critical transition periods in the family life-cycle. The shifts that accompany it are profound, marked, and discontinuous. The new parents are promoted to a different generation. Suddenly they are no longer the young ones, looking only ahead, with their past in the hands of their parents. Suddenly they are moved a step into human history. Most likely, their children will outlive them. Like the death of a parent, the birth of a first child brings with it intimations of the passing of life. It is a reminder of one's own limits, one's own mortality.

The arrival of the first child also joins the new family closer to generational continuity. They are no longer primarily young adults whose major responsibilities are to grow and develop, to separate from their parents, and to look after themselves. Looking after themselves is a bare beginning. They now have to attend to and care for another human being. They have to learn a different way of caring and providing. *Quid pro quo's* worked out to get along in adult relationships do not apply in the same manner to infants and children. Resources of patience, of frustration tolerance, of selflessness, are not only optional and to be rewarded, but are absolutely required day-to-day, with little recognition forthcoming.

Children have membership not only in their immediate nuclear family, but also in two extended families and in various social institutions of the society at large—the neighborhood, the play group, the school, the church. In that sense, parents are guardians of their children. They learn to interact with various social institutions on their children's behalf. So children not only link their parents to their families of origin, they also link them to society at large.

Clinically, difficulties in the family are most frequently noticed at the interfaces of family and other social structures, especially school. Referrals from work situations about family problems are relatively infrequent. They are more frequent in work situations where a good family health-care plan exists and the work world is not totally cut off from the family world. Most of the time, however, the situation is more as described earlier in this chapter. The work world may demand adequate family functioning as a prerequisite, but it does not address family distress.

We do, of course, live in a culture where these kinds of rules and expectations are not clearly defined or agreed upon. So many differences and misunderstandings can arise between families, and even in conflicts between society and the family. In some areas, as with protective vaccinations, society preempts the parents' rights of decision. Other areas, like those of child protection, are less clear.

The arrival of the first child is probably the optimal point of intervention for preventive mental health care. At this time, the marital situation is severely unbalanced. The mother, as well as the father, experience considerable affective lability, a mixture of joy, depression, anxiety, and fatigue. It is, for some families, the only time of hope. It is also a time when new skills have to be learned fast, and a new lifestyle has to be worked out. Families are full of questions, they are open to new learning, eager for help and support. It is a time of high risk for the parents' marriage, and for the newborn. Unlike that later point where parents seek help because something has gone wrong, although we face a new beginning at the first child's birth, parents do not yet feel guilty, discouraged, and worn out.

For the last few years, groups for parents of first-born babies have been forming. This is a new form of service and offers many opportunities for creative development. The involvement of grandparental families, the development of lateral support networks, and the creation of foster extended families are three possible options.

The shift in social role that occurs when a couple become parents for the first time is for the most part, underattended. The advent of the first grandchild may be celebrated, but few thoughts accompany the other implications of the event. There is no special assistance for the new mother, no companionship for the father. There are no experienced teachers at hand to familiarize them with the new tasks. When grandparents are available and willing, other rules often prevent the acceptance of such help. Mental health professionals usually get involved only in the explicit disasters, such as post-partum psychosis. Otherwise, the profession usually contributes little and waits for later disasters to find their way to the therapist's office: the whole range of childhood disorders, disrupted marriages, parental overattachments or underattachments, and boundary problems between family and other social institutions.

The Shift in the Couple

The shift within the couple is, of course, marked. A transition from dyad to triad is required. Exclusive ownership and love, an often cherished fantasy, has to accommodate to sharing, and to limits. The child's needs at times take absolute precedence. The ensuing disappointments are at times blamed on the marital partner. Many parents experience acute jealousy of the time their partner spends with the child and of the pleasure the experience brings. Husbands may not be able to tolerate their wife's breastfeeding, and mothers may get their sexual and maternal feelings mixed up. Nursing the baby may be experienced as too pleasurable to enjoy, or it may temporarily be preferable to sex with the husband. One parent, less anxious than the other, or less tired, may have an easier time calming the baby or putting him to sleep and competitive problems of adequacy and guilt may arise. Both parents experience increased stress, increased work load, lack of sleep. Anxiety about money may also be added, since financial costs are up and income may be down.

Whatever the couple's ideological position, sex-role differentiations have to be worked out. Balances based on egalitarian arrangements have to be rethought. The physical differences in pregnancy, in birth, in nursing, are undeniable and have to be accommodated. This was stated graphically by the wife of a couple who were preparing for parenthood: "I have to attend to it. I am pregnant 24 hours a day. My husband can walk out of the house, perhaps go away for a weekend, and forget about the fact that he will be a father. He can put that role out of his mind. No matter what I do, my belly is right there."

Financial contributions and responsibilities have to be rethought. Looking after a baby takes time, and the time must be taken. Who will take it? Whose career is more flexible? Allows more neglect? Is more important? How important is money and climbing up the income scale?

Other accommodations shift. The adult world of romance is invaded. Different kinds of affection are experienced. Different nurture has to be given. Different priorities affect schedules and activities. Ideas about how contributions are balanced out, an accounting that demands fairly even contributions from both marriage partners, are challenged by the inclusion into the family of a totally unequal little human being. More differentiated solutions have to be sought.

The Family Network

Within the wider family perspective, the arrival of the first child places the young family into historic continuity with the two family lines of each parent. The new arrival has membership in both family networks. This membership is irrevocable, and makes the linkage of the two families irrevocable. The spelling out of these facts is important, especially at a time when the wide prevalence of divorce reshapes the nuclear family. It does not reshape the gnerational family lines. It may well be that an increased awareness of them will help maintain the identity of children whose parents no longer live together.

Sometimes this leads to an actual increase of closeness between the two family networks. Sometimes this does not happen, and membership for the new baby may be actively sought, and/or actively claimed, only within one of the networks. Sometimes the young couple may purchase entry into a family network through their child. Problems may arise when the two families or origin of the parents are in some way very unequal. Perhaps only one accepted the marriage, while the other objected and perhaps refused to recognize it. Perhaps one of the families is seen as vastly preferable by the couple, both of whom agree to limit their allegiance to that family. This can happen when one family is particularly more affluent than the other, or more welcoming, or more attractive, or less trouble ridden. Such a choice may be acceptable to the parental couple. Often, however, it brings in its wake a skewed balance within the family. The parent with the less favored family may feel inferior, less entitled, less worthy, less powerful. The children, in turn, may absorb a whole set of attitudes that accompany this kind of accommodation, without awareness of the context in which they originated. In this sense, attitudes and identities are acquired that can best be understood through a historic view of family and generational transactions.

The first grandchild often brings about an increased closeness with grandparents who claim their part of the baby. Grandparental help is often needed and welcome; grandparental intereference causes troubles. Conflicts are activated and rivalries stirred. Issues of social class, religious affilitation, and family customs, often are sharpened.

Individual Perspective

From the personal perspective of the couple a big step toward maturity was forced upon them. To the extent that they learn to be parents, they relinquish an egocentric position. They learn to see the child as a separate being, and in the process strengthen their own sense of autonomy. In dealing with the child's impulses, they learn to control their own. They find themselves in the position of Janus, each face turned in opposite directions: parents to their child, child to their parents. It is a chance to learn relativity, complementarity; to rediscover some eternal parent-child truth; to reevaluate their relationship to their own parents, now that they are parents themselves.

Most of us start with the notion that we will do things better than our parents. We will not repeat their mistakes. It is even more disturbing to find ourselves making the same mistakes our parents made, those mistakes we hated them for. Or in avoiding those mistakes we make new ones. Despite our best intentions, we are not perfect parents. We hurt our children, we disappoint them, sometimes we don't understand them. Perhaps, then, our parents were not so uncaring either; perhaps they were as well-meaning and conscientious as we are. From this, we take an added step in personal growth—we relinquish blaming our parents for the miseries in our lives and assume that responsibility ourselves.

Of course, parenthood just gives the opportunity for this growth. Although each parent has to move somewhat along this developmental sequence, they do it to differing degrees. What factors influence this growth process is another issue, and another topic. It is a process that can be facilitated in therapy, specifically in therapy that can call on a familiarity with the three areas outlined here: the world of infancy and childhood, the world of adult autonomy, and the world of family transactions.

REFERENCES

Mahler, M.S., Pine, F., & Bergman, A. The psychological birth of the human infant. New York, Basic Books, 1975.

John K. Pearce, M.D.

7
Ethnicity and Family Therapy: An Introduction

This chapter addresses the practical consequences of cultural patterns for psychotherapy. Five objections to this approach are often suggested by thoughtful colleagues. I agree, in part, with these obections, and would like to acknowledge them before the main work of this chapter, the consideration of particular cultural groups and the special problems each may pose for psychotherapists.

1. "Stereotypes are bad."

It is true that ethnic stereotypes have been, and probably always will be, involved in an enormous amount of evil. Furthermore, when we try to make constructive use of ethnic stereotypes that include, as they must, unflattering material, we may add to prejudice. Therapists are better served by learning about the more appealing and constructive sides of a culture, knowledge of strengths; but in order to be effective, we must also be aware of difficulties, particularly cultural values that conflict with those of the therapist's own culture and those values taken for granted in psychotherapy as it is usually practiced. For example, in peasant societies "truth" is not seen as a tool that gives one greater power, and the expression of spontaneous feeling is not usually considered desirable (Spiegel, 1971). Ignorance of cultural patterns is probably the biggest single deficiency in the training of psychotherapists. In spite of real dangers, it should not continue to be neglected.

2. "We are all experts on ethnicity."

We are all experts on at least some cultural patterns. In our homes, growing up, we learn our own culture. When we marry, we are very likely to be confronted with a spouse at least somewhat different, sometimes very different from ourselves. We may have close friends who are particularly important to us because they come from different cultures that have something to teach us about how to live. As an adult, with a spouse and children, each of us tries to create a synthesis, a life drawn from the traditions of our past, but also adding something new that we believe is uniquely right for us. (In time we will learn about the inevitable problems generated by our synthesis.)

We are expert in what we know firsthand. But when we are ignorant of what cultures we may not even be aware of it, and our ignorance may be close to total. We may be ignorant of a conspicuous and omnipresent people like black Americans, about whom, with moderate effort, we can find an immense descriptive literature (Gutman, 1976). Or we may be ignorant about a people we have hardly noticed, like the Azore Islands' Portuguese in my community, Cambridge, Massachusetts. Research on the Portuguese is only beginning, and diligent search will reveal few books (McGill, 1978). Or we even may be ignorant about a people we think we know well, like the American Irish. At least among psychotherapists, the Irish are usually not understood (Organidis & Pearce, 1979).

When we are ignorant, our patients usually don't tell us. There are three reasons why:

1. few people are self-conscious enough to explain themselves in that way. In anthropological field work it is well known that good informants are marginal people. They are aware of the rules of their culture because they see it from the fringe.
2. American melting-pot ideology has discouraged ethnic pride and identity.

3.   The therapist, particularly in individual sessions, has, more than he realizes, the upper hand, and patients try hard to fit into his framework.

It is for this reason that my paper, which is really equally pertinent to individual psychotherapy, was inspired by problems in the practice of family therapy. When the therapist faces an entire family, his power is less and he cannot ignore family values. Furthermore, since a family crisis implicitly challenges both established values and power arrangements, everyone is on the spot. A family may well be more rigid than usual; certainly they'll be more defensive in protecting their values.

3. "It's old stuff."

This work is based on correlation of clinical experience with the readily available literature of anthropology, history, sociology, theology, drama, poetry, and fiction. I particularly draw upon the pioneering work of John Spiegel (1971, 1979) and John Papajohn (Papajohn & Spiegel, 1975). In that sense, it's nothing really new.

In psychiatry we are rightly enthralled with the new. We await the results of new studies in biological psychiatry and family research with hope and enthusiasm. Novel conceptualizations and therapeutic techniques are stimulating and, when we learn to recognize their appropriate range of application, of practical use clinically. But whatever people are has evolved out of what they were, the past. Contemporary conventional social science research is conducted, and it is interesting and legitimate, but it tends mostly to confirm what we knew, not really to surprise us.

From a personal standpoint, the study of ethnicity generates constant surprises and fresh insights. Although what I need to know is in books, I find that I cannot learn about a new culture without the challenge of a live patient, either an individual or a family. Nor can I learn enough directly from my patients. I undertake a dialectic in which I feed back to my patients what I have been learning from my readings. My patients confirm or reject what I offer and are stimulated to look freshly at themselves and their origins.

My practice brings me people from cultures that are new to

me, always something new. A new culture stimulates years of study. The more I learn, the more able I am to find useful materials and fresh insights. Obviously there is no end to these studies.

4. "Culture is superficial."

Psychodynamicists protest that cultural forces are weak compared with intrapsychic instinctual forces. Everyone respects those forces and the psychodynamic models that have evolved in psychoanalytic literature. They are deep and important truths, and appear to be close to universal. But these truths are mediated through cultural and family patterns. For example, many sons, perhaps all, have reason to be deeply angry at their mothers. In some cultures it's all right to be angry at one's mother, particularly within the context of psychotherapy, where it is understood that such feelings should be expressed. But the therapist who waits patiently to hear about an Irishman's rage at his mother will have a very long wait indeed; it is neither allowable nor seen as a pathway to anything constructive. The anger is kept out of mind. The wise therapist approaches that anger through the culturally acceptable pathway of humor: the double message that both acknowledges and denies. Or the therapist might say ironically (and acceptably), "It is a fine thing that you don't get mad at your mother! Not allowed." The rule is made explicit and the hidden truth is implied.

Cultural influences are both superficial and deep. At the surface, where therapist first meets patient, cultural insights are of critical importance in establishing an appropriate therapeutic alliance; e.g., if a Hispanic father wants his child's behavior changed, he has not necessarily agreed to understand how parental alienation has shaped his child's disobedience, but, as a good father, he may be prepared to obey a structural family therapist's task assignments (Minuchin, 1974).

Cultural insights go deep in our understanding the structuring of cognition and affect. For example, an Irish woman from a large, lively family cannot by her own initiative reach out for pleasure. She is a caretaker. She is accustomed to enjoy, indeed has always depended on the pleasure-seeking initiatives of her brothers and her boy friends. Her own efforts always go into endless, often fruitless, caretaking. Both she and her family approve of her caretaking efforts; they fit the Irish cultural pattern. But there is, of course, more, the story; her mother was alcoholic and she is ambivalently identified with her mother's tragic, gradual self-destruction. The psychodynamic and cultural patterns are profoundly interdependent.

5. "People really are all different."

Cultural stereotypes are simple compared to the complexity and variety of real families. Indeed, I think the most striking lesson to be drawn from experience in family therapy is the fantastic variety of families and individuals. How can we relate the actual variety to the relative simplicity of a stereotype? I think that the practical answer is that once having learned it, we should forget about the stereotype, just as we forget about diagnostic or psychodynamic stereotypes. We see real people as directly as we can, but in the back of our minds we scan for patterns. Then, whatever pattern that we think that we see, we test out by using it as a map for further exploration. (In fact, ethnic stereotypes are primarily guides for remembering, straw men on whom we drape the patterns of values we find in cultures.)

No person really fits a stereotype. Because of the normal variety within every culture, the effects of acculturation, and the intermarriage that is practically ubiquitous in our society, only some traditional elements of a single culture are likely to be found in a real person. Often they are parts of a person that are quite taken for granted and unlikely to have been singled out and explained to the therapist, but still important for the therapist to notice. For example, a second-generation Italian woman, preparing to harden her heart in order to break off a relationship with her WASP boy friend, most fears that he will think her heartless. In fact, his complaint about her is that her heart rules her head. What she fears is determined by her Italian values, not by the reality.

SPECIFIC GROUPS

At this point I will turn to particular cultural groups and the special problems each may pose for psychotherapists. I will say most about the Irish, and much less about the Italians, Franco-Americans, WASPs, and Jews.

The Irish

Beginning with the mid-19th century Irish potato famine, the major immigrations to the United States were movements of oppressed people (Woodham-Smith, 1963). Particularly the Irish and Southern Italians were desperately poor; they had experienced savage exploitation that generated deep suspicion toward outside authority (Gambino, 1974). The cultural consequences of oppression must be kept constantly in mind as we consider these and similar cultures. In addition to hostility and suspicion toward outsiders (among whom we psychotherapists must include ourselves), these people possessed the values found in peasant cultures everywhere: conservatism; a sense that the goods of the world were limited, and that one's possession of more goods meant that someone else had less (the principal of the limited good); a sense that nothing could be done about cruel fate and adverse conditions except the bearing of them; and an orientation to present time rather than to the future (Spiegel, 1971). In particular, the great Irish immigration was made up mostly of the poorest peasants, skilled only in potato growing (they had lived and prospered on 10 pounds of potatoes and a half cup of milk a day). They were participants in a society that was the poorest and least touched by the forces of reformation, urbanization, and industrialization of any in Europe (Woodham-Smith, 1963).

But rather than attempt a general account of Irish culture and history, I will shift to the particular troubles that a family therapist is likely to have as he tries to do therapy with an Irish-American family.* Suppose that a multigeneration Irish family has been sent to his office. It is likely they come because they have been told that they should; they are obedient and wish to be seen as people who do the "right" thing. It is likely that they are very doubtful that the therapist will help much, and they assume that if he does it, it will be because of direct, morally oriented advice.

The therapist starts reasonably enough with the question, "What's the trouble?" They answer, but are evasive and give minimal responses. They are particularly reluctant to admit their

---

*For a general account of Irish culture and history, see Arensberg (1968); Arensberg & Kimball (1968); Costigan (1970), Greeley (1972), Orfanidis & Pearce (1979), O'Brien & Conor (1972), and Uris (1976).

trouble, what they see as their "badness," across generational lines within the family. The therapist must be very tactful, emphasize the "normality" of the problem, if possible, and perhaps attribute the problems in a general way to the sinfulness of the times. For more realistic talk, the therapist may have to meet with fewer people: the parents, a group of siblings, or perhaps just one person.

Frustrated in his initial efforts, the therapist who was trained in expressive techniques, like family sculpture, might suggest sculpturing or a role-playing exercise: they won't do it. Why? They know that if they do, the truth will out, and they fear the truth. They do not believe that the truth will make them free; they believe that the truth will show how bad they are and how richly they deserve the trouble they have. They hope to conceal their badness, or that the therapist won't notice, or will be polite enough not to say anything embarrassing. They know the rules. In fact, in Irish families, the primary emphasis is on the rules, which they follow hoping to avoid blame. Everyone keeps his distance; there's not much praise.

I once asked a family group in therapy, "Do you praise the children?" The mother, anxious to show that she did the right thing, replied, "All the time. Kevin here, for example, he's not so bad." Then they laughed, aware that "he's not so bad" was faint praise.

Parents feel that praise "spoils" children. The Catholic Church and its parochial schools perpetuate and elaborate the emphasis on inner badness, particularly the badness of having sexual thoughts which, of course, are unavoidable except by the most drastic repression. The children, in turn, try to conceal their badness. Irish brought up in this tradition *know* that they are bad. This is a key point, maybe the most useful point in this chapter: The therapist must understand about his patients' concealed badness. Although they hope that he will not notice, they will see him as something of a fool if he does not. Acknowledgement of badness is a very sensitive, private matter and the therapist must be tactful. The matter may be brought up in individual sessions, but not in "public," that is, in front of the family.

Counterbalancing the oppressive weight of badness is the *dream,* another key concept for understanding the Irish. George Bernard Shaw in his play, *John Bull's Other Island,* describes

Irish dreaming—here speaks Laurence Doyle, Civil Engineer and Irishman:

> No, no: the climate is different. Here (in England) if the life is dull, you can be dull too, and no great harm done. (Going off into a passionate dream). But your wits can't thicken in that soft moist air, on those white springy roads, in those misty rushes and brown bogs, on those hillsides of granite rocks and magenta heather. You've no such colors in the sky, no such lure in the distances, no such sadness in the evenings. Oh, the dreaming! the dreaming! the torturing, heart-scalding, never satisfying dreaming, dreaming, dreaming, dreaming! (Savagely) No debauchery that ever coarsened and brutalized an Englishman can take the worth and usefulness out of him like that dreaming. An Irishman's imagination never lets him alone, never convinces him, never satisfies him; but it makes him that he can't face reality not deal with it, nor handle it, nor conquer it: he can only sneer at them that do, and (bitterly) be "agreeable to strangers," like a good-for-nothing woman on the street. It's all dreaming, all imagination. He can't be religious. The inspired Churchman that teaches him the sanctity of life and the importance of conduct is sent away empty; while the poor village priest that gives him a miracle or a sentimental story of a saint, has cathedrals built for him out of the pennies of the poor. He can't be intelligently political: he dreams of what the Shan Van Vocht said in ninety-eight. If you want to interest him in Ireland you've got to call the unfortunate island Kathleen ne Hoolihan and pretend she's a little old woman. It saves thinking. It saves working. It saves everything except imagination, imagination, imagination, and imagination's such a torture that you can't bear it without whisky. (With fierce, shivering, self-contempt) At last you get that you can bear nothing real at all: you'd rather starve than cook a meal; you'd rather go shabby and dirty than set your mind to take care of your clothes and wash yourself; you nag and squabble at home because your wife isn't an angel, and she despises you because you're not a hero; and you hate the whole lot round you because they're only poor slovenly useless devils like yourself. . . .

Deep conviction of badness is escaped in dreaming, and dreaming takes away the possibility of directly engaging and testing reality (which in the previous 300 years in Ireland has been grim). A direct encounter with emotional conflict is resisted.

I recall a demonstration family interview conducted by Nathan Ackerman at Massachusetts Mental Health Center in the late 60s. It was a familiar Irish family constellation: a peripheral, alcoholic father; a depressed, withdrawn teenage son who was refusing to go to school and staying home in his room; and a suffering, dutiful mother. Ackerman deftly drew out into the open the emotional issues. He showed that the son was paralyzed by his ambivalence toward his mother. He couldn't live out his mother's dream that he be the "good one" who made her dreams come true, nor could he be like his father, his disappointing father. He could not rebel against the entire situation, so he withdrew into depression. It was a brilliant interview. But when the family's social worker met with the family the next day, they could remember nothing of the interview. The direct encounter was forgotten. It is not effective.

Another useful example of the interplay of badness, dreaming, and denial is the action in Eugene O'Neill's *Long Day's Journey Into Night*. When, in the play, the cruel truths tumble into the open, when the dreams are attacked, then from the mouths of the family members repeatedly come denials and disqualifications: "Let's forget me" "I'm not interested in the subject, neither are you." "Christ! That's a lousy thing to say, I don't mean that." "You damned fool! No one was to blame." "All right, Mama, I'm sorry I spoke." "I didn't think anything!" On and on it goes. The family tries to face the truth, but they are overwhelmed by their badness and the empty allure of their dreams. It is particularly noteworthy that, although all of the characters do know the truth, they set it aside for the sake of someone else. They try to protect each other's dreams. It is not denial as an unconscious defense, but denial as moral policy (Netsky, 1978).

Why the denial? Spiegel (1979) describes how Irish children are taught the rules with a technique he calls "confession extraction." For example, if a mother comes home to find the cookie jar broken she angrily accuses each child in turn, "You broke the jar!" Each is expected to either protest innocence indignantly or confess guilt tearfully. The real point the mother makes is not that she cares about the jar, or that children should never raid cookie jars and break them, it is that the children should know and respect the rule ("don't raid the cookie jar").

Although open moral condemnation is avoided in front of strangers, as in the initial family interview, when the provocation is sufficient, punishment can be public and severe: e.g., an Irish boy had been arrested for a juvenile offense, thereby seriously embarrassing the family. Although defiant toward the police, the boy, hearing that his mother had arrived at the police station, pleaded with the juvenile officer, "Please don't let her hurt me!" The mother, ordinarily polite and respectful, entered the room and smacked him across the face. He had gone too far (Orfanidis, 1978).

Is there any escape from the burden of sin? There is, of course, confession, penance, and absolution on a short-term basis; but only death promises hope for final release, and even then it is a sin of presumption to feel sure that one is saved.

There is felt to be a hidden moral order that punishes the wicked. There is a familiar saying: "He'll get his!" Every evil-doer will be punished. Knowing that he too is bad, that he too will "get his," an Irishman who fails in his dreams (loses his job, fails in an ambition, etc.) feels, although he loudly protests his innocence, that he's getting what he truly deserves; perhaps even less punishment than he deserves. He may not try really hard to get out of his difficulties because, as another popular saying puts it, "The devil you know is better than the devil you know not!" If you escape one punishment, you get another, maybe worse. When defeated in their dreams, Irishmen and women may withdraw into chronic depression, "Bog melancholy" (Alfred, 1978; Dunne, 1977). Christ-like, they offer up their suffering as a gift to God.

Hogan's Goat, William Alfred's powerful tragic play portrays the sequence of sin, the dream, failure as punishment, and final ruin. The story: Matthew Stanton, a politician in Brooklyn, had, as a very young man, secretly married a disreputable woman. Later in life, he bigamously married a saintly young woman who knew nothing of his past. A political scandal gives him an opportunity to gain advantage by betraying his close friend, the incumbent Mayor of Brooklyn, and to run for Mayor of Brooklyn himself with a good chance of winning. (Treason is a dreaded, familiar, and despicable crime in Irish tradition because of the insidious efforts of the English to buy their supporters and to encourage and exploit disloyalty.) His past is unearthed, his political career is ruined; his dream is destroyed. To keep his wife, who now knows all, from leaving him, he pushes her down the stairs, hoping to break her leg or otherwise disable her for a while. The fall breaks her back and kills her. He's led off to jail in tears, and the priest has the last word, "Well, you may cry! Cry for us all while you're at it. Cry for us all!"

I have made prospects for the therapy look bleak. Problems

are greatest in the family session, but they are also serious in the individual sessions. In order to conduct psychoanalytically-oriented therapy, the patient must see some point in uncovering the truth. But as we have seen, truth is more than usually threatening.

The stance that the therapist assumes toward the patient can be a problem, too. As a rule, psychotherapists are trained to assume a stance similar to that of a physician, or a clergyman, or a rabbi, or perhaps a scientific investigator. None of these are really satisfactory for treating the Irish. (The role of priest is an obvious possibility, but I know not a single therapist, not even a former priest, who finds that a useful stance. There are certainly psychotherapists who are priests, but I don't know any.) The relationship that does make sense to the Irish is "friendship" (Arensberg, 1968), a form of relationship traditionally avoided by therapists. In Ireland, "friendship" was the primary social bond; all officially endorsed and bureaucratic relationships were the creatures of alien English law, despised by the Irish people and ignored.* The therapist is, or can be, a friend. The traditional problem with the friendship relationship for patient and therapist is the lack of clear boundaries and role limitations. This does not seem to be a problem in Irish friendships; they are courtly, well-ordered, warm, but limited relationships. I have never had a problem with an Irishman "taking advantage" of friendship. More usual is the example of my patient with a serious sleep disturbance, about whom I would like to keep well informed, who said, "I'll call you if I really get desperate." The core rules of friendship are obligatory loyalty and respectful friendliness. (All this does not apply to an Irishman who has been drinking. The rules are suspended, and he is best avoided.)

If, as we have seen, the Irish know that they are bad, then what is the therapist? He's bad too. The Irish are accustomed to hypocrisy, and they will pretend that the therapist is "good." It is a futile game, and best avoided. The therapist might instead say (only in an individual session, of course), "Ah, I can see that

*In fact it was the English persecution of Catholic priests in the time of the Cromwellian slaughter (mid-17th century) that bound the Irish people to them and made the church the first unifying national force that much-conquered Ireland had known (Greeley, 1972).

you're a bad one." The patient indignantly replies, "What makes you think I'm bad?" The therapist counters, "It takes one to know one." The patient laughs at the wit and the ironic confirmation of what the patient, in fact, never doubted. On occasion the therapeutic alliance may be that of two flawed souls conspiring to get by in a hard world. The therapist might ask incredulously, "You thought that you had to be *worthy* to get a Ph.D.? Your professors are saints? They're flawed like us! Besides, it's embarrassing to the department when graduate students don't finish their theses?" The "demonic therapeutic alliance" probably works best when patient and therapist are the same sex. Women are supposed to be different, better than men (Warner, 1976), and they find it hard to drop the stance in the company of a male therapist. Apparently a female therapist can work along these lines with a man (Keller, 1978).

Women, as I mentioned, are better, but they pay for their moral superiority. In *Games Alcoholics Play,* Claude Steiner (1971) describes a drinking pattern, "Drunk and Proud Of It," that is typically (though far from exclusively) Irish: He feels inferior to her. In retaliation he gets drunk and abuses her. The next morning, moaning with pain, his head splitting, he begs her forgiveness: "Forgive me honey, I swear-to-God I"ll never do it again." If she forgives him, he wins because he's tricked her; he's got his forgiveness and he can still get drunk anytime he pleases. If she refuses to forgive, he wins; "She won't forgive me," he thinks to himself, "she's not so good." Her only way out is to refuse to judge him. Refraining from judging nor forgiving obviously does not come easily to the Irish.

A therapeutic way of dealing with badness that is remarkably helpful is the assignment of a task, the performance of "ceremonies of badness." For example, upwardly mobile Irish couples who feel terribly guilty about their good fortune are vulnerable to episodes of mutual accusations that are an attempt to externalize their inner sense of badness onto their spouse. They fight bitterly. In the therapeutic task, they are instructed to set aside a special time when they are to ironically, absurdly, and ceremoniously accuse each other of badness. After the "ceremony" they experience diminished inner sense of superego pressure and are astonished to recognize what they had actually been thinking. Consider, for example, an academic couple: "Her" book had just been accepted for publication by an important publisher and she was anxiously elated. "He" said, "When they find out how bad you are they'll change their mind and turn it down." She gasped, "You know, that's what I really thought." They found that the ceremony decreased their fights, and they were as surprised as I was that it actually worked.

I want to point out that although this is a paradoxical intervention it's usefulness does not depend on oppositional trends within the patients. The primary effect seems to be intrapsychic. It is also true, however, that, like a strategic family therapist in requesting that they carry out an important interpersonal sequence in a different context, I am chancing the way that such a sequence would occur spontaneously (Haley, 1973; Rabkin, 1977).

Gestalt therapists are successful in doing emotionally expressive therapy with Irish young adults (Blatt, 1975). It is instructive to see how they do it—in a group setting in which the norm is emotional expression; where enormous pressure is exerted (the "hot seat"); where there is the illusion of freedom to participate or not ("Would you like to work tonight?"), yet no way to not participate ("Why are you in this group if you don't want to work?"); and where there is overwhelming group approval and support (for example, the therapist may ask each member of the group to tell the person in the "hot seat" something they like about him/her)—under these conditions of maximum pressure and support, traditional expressive therapy apparently works well. (Of course, some Irish patients will readily take to expressive therapy under any conditions.)

Although the expressive-interpretative approach is problematic, behavior modification with an emphasis on giving detailed directions, strategic therapy aimed at highly enmeshed oppositional families, the intergenerational loyalty family therapy of Boszormenyi-Nagy & Spark (1973) with an emphasis on loyalty and the calculus of obligations—most other family therapy approaches—work well. The Bowen Therapy (Bowen, 1978; Guerin, 1976) is, however, by far the best suited to Irish families. Murray Bowen sees the fundamental problem in families as interpersonal fusion. The process of cure involves establishing differentiated person-to-person relationship with as many members as possible of the extended family. Bowen's theory holds that in a multigenerational process, some children are selected, and self-

selected, to be overinvolved with parents. They are restricted by
anxiety, and familial constraints that generate anxiety, in their
ability to think clearly about choices and to take stands in order
to try out new behaviors. They are not able to distinguish between thinking and emotional reactions, or to choose to act on the
basis of thinking. When the patient in Bowen therapy is able to
consistently establish thinking-oriented relationships with family members, to not react emotionally to the opposition within the
family system to his unwillingness to participate in scapegoating
and "cut-offs," then, after monumental fuss, other people start to
behave more sensibly, too.

The values implicit in this therapy fit Irish culture right
down the line: loyalty to the family (working out relationships
within the family), calm thinking rather than emotional display,
individual responsibility and initiative, and even heroic action
(taking on the family in this way is a heroic undertaking). An
additional plus is the healing of "cut-offs." In typically small and
isolated Irish villages, people were tied together by bonds of obligatory friendliness and interdependence. One's margin of survival was too slim to do without a friend's help, and to not be
spoken to was the utlimate social sanction. In America, economic
necessity no longer kept people cooperating, so that an Irishman
could afford to quarrel, project his badness on someone else (his
brother, for example), and cut off communication. This happens
often. The Bowen approach considers healing such cut-offs as particularly important.

Acculturation has been remarkably slow in changing Irish
working-class communities in the big cities. The Irish didn't have
to learn a new language (although many did speak only Gaelic
when they came to America); they established their own churches
and schools; they see their values as being "American;" and they
are not really aware that they are different. Acculturation
primarily occurs with upward mobility, movement to non-Irish
neighborhoods, attendance at non-Catholic schools, and entry
into non-Irish professions (like psychiatry). Irishmen often come
to therapy both as a result of and as part of the acculturation
process moving them toward dominant American middle-class
values. They find therapy difficult. Progress is slow, and the
therapist must be patient. If he can be content with gradual progress, he will be rewarded with rich experience.

There is no one book that summarizes what is important to know about the Irish; they are not fond of explaining themselves. A book like James Carroll's *Mortal Friends* is a good example: Carroll, an ex-Jesuit Priest, tells a tale that exemplifies what happens in two generations of acculturation, but he does not spell it out explicitly. On the other hand, Leon Uris, the Jewish American writer, takes the time in *Trinity* to *explain* history, and *Trinity* is probably the best book for beginning study of the Irish (Warner, 1976).

The Italians

The Italians, however, have a great book: *Blood of My Blood* by Richard Gambino. This book is indispensible for therapists who see Italian patients (that is, all therapists). It is equally useful to patients. A word of warning: *Blood of My Blood* exemplifies an important trait—it gets you whole-heartedly on the side of the Italians—that is valuable, because, as I have said, appreciation is what is most useful to the therapist; but Gambino does not prepare his readers for the darker side of Italian life.

A general principle is that Italians come to therapists intending to get them on their side. A therapeutic stance of neutrality and objectivity is likely to be seen as hostile and is useless. Italians draw their boundaries tightly and regard outsiders as enemies. In confiding, they let you in. You must be on their side. In my experiences this is not an arrangement that binds me, a trap; however, inasmuch as I prize impartiality, it still makes me uneasy. As I learn more about the family, I can be on several people's sides at once; they all have points of view with which one can be sympathetic.

There is a story about the wise Rabbi of Lublin, who had a reputation as an accomplished marriage counselor. Once an unhappy wife approached him and, after she had told her sad story, he said, "You're absolutely right." Then her husband appeared and told his story. "You're absolutely right," said the Rabbi. His student witnessed both conversations and took him to task saying, "You tell her she's right; you tell him he's right; it doesn't make sense!" The Rabbi replied, "You're absolutely right." (Each one had a legitimate point of view.)

An important problem with any form of therapy with Italian

men, but particularly with family therapy, is that Italian men are likely to engage in a dominance struggle with a male therapist. The therapist must be ceremoniously respectful of the husband's dignity. But even then, with great respect shown, the Italian man may have to show that the therapist is wrong and useless. It may even be the case that the Italian must go and find a second and even more useless therapist before he will feel that he can make use of what he learned from the first. Women therapists do better; there is no need for a dominance struggle. But even they have trouble if their status is too high: one of my colleagues, Lucia Antonioli, did well with Italian families until she became director of the day hospital in which she worked. Then she found that her importance made her a threat to the men and led to dominance conflicts.

What is one to do in individual and family therapy with Italians? Traditional expressive therapy with an individual probably works acceptably, but with couples or families, an expressive or communications approach won't do. They know how to express their feelings, and truth in itself is viewed with suspicion. The core family value (as Gambino emphasizes) is *tradition*. Tradition has many sides and there is room for disagreement, but it is vital that the therapist use the word ("tradition") and show primary respect for tradition.

Family systems approaches, either Bowen's or Boszormenyi-Nagy's, work well. There are some hitches: In the Bowen approach it is supposed that everyone should be cool. In a traditional Italian family a man is supposed to be cool and dignified until things have gotten too far out of hand, then he is supposed to blow his top. A woman who doesn't lose emotional control when suitably provoked would be seen as unloving and untraditional. No heart.

Again and again I make the same point: any treatment method must harmonize with the values of the clinical population to which it will be applied. (What could be more obvious?) The Irish esteem the coolness that the Italians would see as heartless. I do not mean that the Bowen approach won't work with Italians; on the contrary, in other ways the matching of values is very close; but in that one way it must be modified.

There is a more general point: to properly understand any therapy, one must look at it squarely within the cultural setting in which it arises—e.g., psychoanalysis sprang from turn of the century Vienna—and then you must trace its development in the various cultural settings in which it flourishes—e.g., psychoanalysis as it spread through Europe and was modified in America—and then you must look at it as it is today—who are the patients? who is helped? who is not helped, or harmed? Only then can a rational ecological perspective on psychotherapies emerge.

Franco-Americans

The Irish and Italians came to America in force and have been conspicuous for their achievements since they came. The situation of the French in Canada and America is different. They have been here longer than anyone (1608, the settlement of Quebec), but are relatively invisible. It is only recently, since World War Two, that their young men, having learned better English and about more lucrative work opportunities, have moved from French-speaking, socially isolated communities into the main stream of American life. Their isolated culture had been shaped and given boundaries by their authoritarian French Catholic Church, their poverty, their profound sense of oppression by outsiders, their bitterness at having been abandoned by France, and their pride in the French language and their spiritual superiority (Hughes, et al., 1960).

The core values of Franco-American families seem to be hard work and having a warm and supportive family. Like the Irish, the women tend to group together around domestic interests, while the men separate from them to drink and follow sports. Children are not taught about psychological problems. In fact, psychotherapeutic efforts with Franco-Americans must begin, and perhaps be limited, to education, particularly about the management of anger and aggression. Acting up (or "out" if you prefer) is taken for granted. Conventional psychotherapy usually fails. Therapists are unhappy about this and end up saying that these patients are "primitive." They are not, but they must be taught a great deal more about what we want and the useful things we can understand about them.

It is possible to conduct whole or extended family sessions if the therapist focused on matters that harmonize with the value of having a warm and supportive family, e.g., finding how family members are attempting to help each other and making plans for future support. Approaches that rely on stimulating conflict, like network therapy (Speck & Attneave, 1973), may be disastrous. Because of the tradition of obedience to a strong and present church, they will submit to authority; but their unfamiliarity with being called to acknowledge psychological problems and their tendency to scapegoat outsiders (you) and manage tensions by action (drinking, fighting, gambling, etc.) can create conditions in which the therapist will get into situations he will regret.

WASPs

There are all kinds of white Anglo-Saxon Protestants (WASPs), and, of course, many of them aren't descendents of the Anglo or Saxon germanic tribes that invaded England in the fifth century. The acronym WASP usually refers to white Protestants who are at least fairly well-to-do. WASP subcultures range from the upper-class Brahmins (from all over the East, but traditionally, Boston) to southern gentry, to rednecks, and to the solid citizens of the middle west, (Mead, 1971). They are very different: The Brahmins value nobless oblige and conservation; they look to the past and try to be worthy of it. Upwardly mobile southerners are confused and caught between two other very different traditions: the hard-working, free-thinking, God-fearing, very independent Scotch-Irish redneck tradition, and the aristocratic, dashing, honor-preoccupied Cavalier tradition. The westerners, who were mostly Scotch-Irish (similar, but not quite the same as those who stayed behind in the south and are briefly characterized in the previous paragraph), pushed out through Pennsylvania to pioneer the rest of the United States in the 19th century; they embody familiar values that have been particularly celebrated in Western movies and are certainly important mainstream American values—an emphasis on independent judgement, hard work, being reasonably good, not complaining, facing the truth, looking forward to the future, and trying to be cheerful.

This constellation of values is compatible with all schools of psychotherapy. Because these WASPs love, or at least can love, the truth, and are hopeful about self-improvement and the future (Hale, 1971), they are likely to go to therapy. Although the match is close, there are important conflicts with the value of therapists. Denial is considered a low-level defense, particularly in the psychoanalytic world; but although the WASPs feel that they *must* face the truth, they often don't like it; and cheerful denial as a defense is not incompatible with generally good functioning. WASPs who have been prosperous and secure for several generations are particularly vulnerable to tragic losses because of their use of denial and their lack of a tragic perpsective on life. When children or adults die "before their time," they are crushed, don't know what to make of it. They can be effectively helped by all therapies that respect the importance of mourning, that is, almost all therapies. Thus, a value discrepancy turns out to be a benefit; the WASPs come to therapy in misery, and gain a whole new perspective on their lives.

One distinction that has major implications for therapy is between liberal and evangelical Protestants. Farmers everywhere have a crucial direct relationship with nature and nature's God who punishes sins with rain or drought. Exfarmers who moved to towns where they became prosperous and immune to such forces adopted a new version of Christianity in which the idea of the Second Coming was replaced by the idea of heaven on earth, to be achieved by social and economic progress. It is these people who lost their tragic sense; they are vulnerable not only to tragic loss, but also to the catastrophe or trying to have perfect families. "Perfect" families are vulnerable, tend to be cut off from the wider community, and soon become monsters of pseudomutuality. The farmers who stayed on the land stayed closer to the old religion and evangelical values—each man with his Bible and God's guiding hand could discover God's absolute truth, earthly life was merely preparation for salvation. The inheritors of this tradition look askance at psychology and learning in general. They see it as a new faith corrupting the old; and, of course, they are absolutely right. To treat evangelicals, the therapist must adapt his methods to match evangelical values. (Do I grow tedious? The same message again.) Since the evangelicals see the family as structured like the universe, with God and the father at the top, the therapist must understand and accept that hierarchical assumption: He must affirm that the family has the resources to deal with its own problem. He must not express doubts about the evangelical faith. If the therapist is fortunate enough to know the scriptures (I don't) he can and should quote a Bible text in the service of his cause. In general, his strategy will be reframing; e.g., if the family complaint is about teenage rebellion, what is seen in evangelical terms as a matter of disobedience comparable to disobedience of God, then the problem should be reframed in terms of the importance of encouraging responsibility in young people, another evangelical value (Larsen, 1976).

The Jews

All therapists should be aware of the very great differences between the cultures of the Eastern European Jews (the shtetl), the German Jews who had been acculturated to German culture (Birmingham, 1977) and the Sephardic Jews who were Spaniards and are like other Mediterraneans (Birmingham, 1971).

Life Is With People: The Culture of the Shtetl by Mark Zborowski and Elizabeth Herzog is an outstanding book about life in the Shtetl. Like Gambino, it should be read by patients and therapists alike. In the Jewish ghetto, the shtetl, under circumstances of constant threat and vulnerability from the intermittent pogroms, the men obsessively studied and debated the holy law that, were it properly obeyed, gave the community protection. The covenant agreement obligated God to protect them. An additional pathway to magical security was worrying, particularly on the part of the women. ("God forbid my son should get sick! Oi Vay!") They saw suffering as a kind of work, work that magically protects (Zborowski, 1969). (One can see this value today in the therapists who similarly see suffering in therapy as work of self-evident value.)

German Jews are said to be more like WASPs than WASPs: correct, controlled, thoughtfully intellectual, keenly aware of how they are seen by their neighbors. Of course, they are not WASPs, but they were acculturated as Germans and are a dominant influence in the psychoanalytic movement (Janik, 1973)—analysis is a therapy well-suited to them.

It is ironic that Eric Berne, a German Jew who wrote impeccably compulsive books [for example, Berne (1963)] also founded the Transactional Analysis movement (Berne, 1964). TAs informal terminology, combined with an emphasis on action, the role of the will in producing therapeutic change, and general optimism about the future, has made it a WASP therapy par excellence.

Mixed Marriages

Most marriages are mixed marriages. Unfortunately, spouses tend to perceive their cultural differences as failings— either badness or madness. Insight into the cultural origin of differences is very helpful. With insight, people are able to take some distance from their hurt feelings and stop taking inevitable differences personally.

Big differences are everywhere. Consider how differently something basic like suffering is experienced: The Irishman sees his suffering as punishment for badness; it is deserved and inescapable, but must be nominally protested to avoid admitting that he is bad—Christ-like, he may offer it up as a sacrifice to God. The Jew sees suffering as constructive magical work, and/or an arguing point that God is not holding up his end of the deal. The WASP sees suffering as an obscurely adverse comment on his worth—he hates to face it but he will, particularly if that will help get rid of it. The Franco-American will attempt total denial. The Italian will maintain dignified reserve with outsiders, but may bitterly complain to his family to stimulate the sympathy and help he deserves. Eastern European Catholics expect to suffer and have a fundamental tolerance of their suffering; they don't expect to escape it (Stein, 1978a; 1978b). In clinical practice, with a sharp eye, you see these kinds of things many times a day.

Sometimes the cultural conflicts are isomorphic (same shape) with a psychodynamic conflict. For example, a second generation Jewish wife was furious with her second generation Italian husband for taking the smaller of their two cars on a brief trip. To her, love means avoiding injury—taking the safer car; for him, what was important was that the car had a radio, a source of greater pleasure on the trip. Underneath the cultural difference was a transference issue: she felt that her father didn't really care about her. When the conflict was interpreted in cultural terms, it faded for the moment, but soon came up again in another form. Interpreting the cultural-content level will not push a psychodynamic (or transference) conflict out of sight. On the other hand, initial interpretation of the psychodynamic aspect would, I think, tend to reductionistically block awareness of the cultural conflict, a difference that, understood, should promote differentiation and great richness in the marriage.

CONCLUSION

Having described some of the vast weave of cultural patterns that can be seen in the practice of psychotherapy, and acknowledging the problems of transferences, I want to mention something that remains a vital element that does not altogether yield to reductionistic analysis and is vital to the outcome in our work—that is the everyday quality of relationships, the caring. If a couple (and family) respect and love each other (recognizing that the word "love" is used in a dozen ways) therapy will work well; if not, clarity of understanding will promote break-up.

Virginia Satir (1976) sees this dimension fundamentally as self-esteem. She is herself a genius at making people feel better about themselves; she calls it "filling the pot." She thinks that there are really no important differences between people. As long as their self-esteem is up, as long as the pot is full, then people will get along together. I think that is true. But her perspective and ours needs to be enlarged to recognize that people are different in the ways that the pot can be filled.

REFERENCES

Alfred, W. Hogan's Goat, New York: Noonday Press, 1966.

Alfred, W. (Personal communication) 1978.

Arensberg, C. The Irish countryman. New York: Natural History Press, 1968.

Arensberg, C. M., & Kimball, S.T. Family and community in Ireland. Cambridge: Harvard Press, 1968.

Berne, E. The structure and dynamics of organizations and groups. New York: J.B. Lippincott, 1963.

Berne, E. Games people play. New York: Grove Press, 1964.

Birmingham, S. The grandees: America's Sephardic elite. New York: Harper and Row, 1971.

Birmingham, S. Our crowd. New York: Pocket Book, 1977.

Blatt, M. (Personal communication) 1975.

Boszormenyi-Nagy, I, & Spark, G.M. Invisible loyalties: Reciprocity in intergenerational family therapy. New York: Harper and Row, 1973.

Bowen, M. Family therapy in clinical practice. New York: Jason Aronson, 1978.

Carroll, J. Mortal friends. Boston: Little, Brown, 1978.

Costigan, G. A history of modern Ireland. New York: Pagasus, 1970.

Dunne, J.G. True confessions. New York: E. P. Dutton, 1977.

Gambino, R. Blood of my blood: The dilemma of the Italian-American. Garden City: Doubleday and Co., 1974.

Greeley, A.M. That most distressful nation: The taming of the American Irish. Chicago: Quadrangle Books, 1972.

Guerin, P.J. (Ed.). Family therapy: Theory and practice. New York: Gardner Press, 1976.

Gutman, H.G. The black family. *In* Slavery and freedom 1750–1925. New York: Pantheon Books, 1976.

Hale, N. G. Jr. Freud and the Americans: The beginnings of psychoanalysis in the United States, 1876–1917. New York: Oxford, 1971.

Haley, J. Uncommon therapy: The psychiatric techniques of Milton H. Erickson, M.D. New York: W. W. Norton & Co., 1973.

Hughes, C. C., Trembley, M., Rapoport, R., et al. People of Cove and Woodlot: Communities from the viewpoint of social psychiatry. New York: Basic Books, 1960.

Janik, A., & Toulmin, S. Wittgenstein's Vienna. New York: Simon and Schuster, 1973.

Keller, S. (Personal communication) 1978.

Larsen, J. A. Dysfunction in the evangelical family: Treatment Considerations. Paper presented at meeting of AAMFC, Philadelphia, October, 1976.

McGill, D. (Personal communication) 1978.

Mead, M. And keep your powder dry: An anthropologist looks at America. New York: William Morrow, 1971.

Minuchin, S. Families and family therapy. Cambridge: Harvard University Press, 1974.

Netsky, R. Family dynamics in Eugene O'Neill's *Long Day's Journey Into Night.* Unpublished paper, for copies write Massachusetts Mental Health Center, Boston, 1978.

Orfanidis, M. (Personal communication) 1978.

Orfanidis, M. & Pearce, J. Family Therapy with Irish Americans. Unpublished manuscript, 1979.

O'Brien, M., & Conor, A. A concise history of Ireland. New York: Beekman House, 1972.

Papajohn, J., & Spiegel, J. Transactions in families. San Francisco, Jossey-Bass, 1975.

Rabkin, R. Strategic psychotherapy: Brief and symptomatic treatment. New York: Basic Books, 1977.

Satir, V. Changing the family. Palo Alto: Science and Behavior, 1976.

Shaw, G. B. Collected plays and their prefaces, vol. 2. New York: Dodd, Mead and Co., 1971.

Speck, R. V., and Attneave, C. L. Family networks. New York: Pantheon, 1973.

Spiegel, J. Transactions: The interplay between individual, family and society. *In* Papajohn, J. (Ed.). New York, Science House, 1971.

Spiegel, J. P. Ethnopsychiatric dimensions in family violence. Presented at AAAS annual meeting, Jan 3–8, 1979, Houston, Texas.

Stein, H. F. Aging and Death Among Slovak-Americans. *The Journal of Psychological Anthropology, 1978a, 1,* 297–320.

Stein, H. F. The Slovak-American "Swaddling Ethos": Hoemostat for Family Dynamics and Cultural Persistence. *Family Process,* 1978b, *17,* Number 1.

Steiner, C. Games alcoholics play. New York: Ballantine Books, 1971.

Uris, L. Trinity. Garden City: Doubleday Press, 1976.

Warner, M. Alone of All Her Sex: The myth and the cult of the Virgin Mary. New York: Alfred A. Knopf, 1976.

Woodham-Smith, C. The great hunger. New York: Harper & Row, 1963.

Zborowski, M. People in pain. San Francisco, Jossey-Bass, 1969.

Zborowski, M., & Herzog, E. Life is with people: The culture of the shtetl. New York: Schocken Books, 1976.

Samuel Slipp, M.D.

8
Interactions Between the Interpersonal in Families and Individual Intrapsychic Dynamics

The Symbiotic Survival Pattern is a unifying concept integrating the understanding of intrapsychic functioning derived from psychoanalytic investigations with the newer developments concerning family interaction and systems that have evolved from the family therapy movement. Both the psychoanalytic and the family approaches deal with the same psychiatric phenomena, but from different levels or perspectives. The Symbiotic Survival Pattern provides bridging concepts to bring these two perspectives together into an interactive, interdependent theoretical framework (Slipp, 1973).

THE NEED FOR AN INTERGRATIVE THEORY

The first generation of pioneers in the family therapy movement, like all innovators, met with considerable opposition as they attempted to develop a new conceptual structure. But the family therapy movement is over twenty years old; now it is legitimate. With its viability and identity assured, it need not continue an oppositional struggle against the establishment—the rebellious young Turks have themselves become the graybeards; they are no longer the underdog fighting the power elite. Family therapy has been accepted and is taught in academic and medical centers. It is required in Community Mental Health Centers and as part of child psychiatry training. It is an important part of psychiatric, psychological, social work, and psychoanalytic meetings.

Max Weber, the eminent sociologist, pointed out that innovators, who carved out new territory, were charismatic individuals, larger than life. They are followed by the second generation, who integrate and institutionalize these advances. This is the current situation in family therapy. Recently (1979) its leaders founded the American Family Therapy Association. It is thus appropriate and timely that family therapy is integrated with the existing body of knowledge about mental disorders. We are now growing more and more to accept the fact that causality is more complicated than we had thought. No single discipline can explain causality, which usually requires a combination of factors. In behavioral science we need an interdisciplinary approach that integrates cultural, social, familial, psychological, biological, and genetic factors.

New interdisciplinary fields are being created, for example sociobiology. What hindered the development of these interdisciplinary fields in the behavioral sciences is that each discipline restricted its viewpoint. Levinson (1964) points out that in psychology reality was viewed almost as if it were a "mirage," a product of human personality. On the other hand, sociology advocated a "sponge" theory, discounting human personality, and seeing individuals as passively conforming to group pressures. This dichotomy could never account for unique responses in individuals, such as deviance, growth, change, or creativity. To some extent, this same dichotomy exists in the family therapy field between those adhering to the systems and psychoanalytic approaches. It would be unfortunate if conflict within the field of family therapy continued between these two approaches. Instead, it is imperative that an integration of the various viewpoints occur that will provide an interactive, interdependent framework.

THE MEANING OF "SYMBIOTIC SURVIVAL PATTERN"

Now that the need for an integrative theory has been established, you may wonder why this theory was termed the Symbiotic Survival Pattern. First of all, the name of the theory combines both intrapsychic and interpersonal factors. The identified patient is seen as intrapsychically fixated at the *symbiotic* phase of infantile development. However, this fixation occurs because of, and is perpetuated by, a *continued pattern* of symbiotic relatedness within the family. Thus the term *pattern* is used. This relationship is panphasic and not limited to infantile development, and its purpose is for *survival* of self and others.

Webster defines symbiosis as "the living together in more or less intimate association or even close union of two dissimilar organisms." Ordinarily this relationship is advantageous or necessary to both parties, but not harmful to either. In psychoanalysis, symbiosis describes a normal phase of infantile development. Fixation at this phase may lead to pathological disturbances of body image, ego boundaries, and identity formation. Mahler & Furer (1968) define the normal symbiotic phase of infantile development as existing from about the 3rd to the 18th month of life. It is characterized by an intrapsychic fusion of the images of self and mother. This serves as a defense to deny the infant's separateness and its helplessness. Magically, the infant feels in control of the mother. Its purpose is to insure survival. Jacobson (1967) and others consider that in schizophrenia, the patient is fixated at this symbiotic phase of development. When regression occurs, the ego boundaries between self and the other disappear, accompanied by an intrapsychic fustion of these images. In manic depressive psychosis, Fromm-Reichmann (1959) and others consider the fixation point to be between the resolution of the symbiotic phase and the initiation of the separation-individuation phase. Here the other is no longer seen as a part-object, but as a whole and separate individual. Thus in depression, the fear of abandonment by the other becomes a primary concern.

PREVIOUS FORMULATIONS

The unique contribution of family studies has been to demonstrate, both experimentally and clinically, that the family exerts continuing influence on the patient's functioning long past infancy and early childhood. This has been particularly studied with schizophrenics who are still living with their families of origin. Many family investigators have described the family's interference with individuation and separation of these patients.

Wynne et al (1958) termed this family process, "pseudo-mutuality." The family maintains a facade of togetherness, but at the expense of individual differentiation of identities. Bowen (1960) termed a similar process the "undifferentiated family ego mass"; Lidz et al (1965) reported on the disruption of normal boundaries within the family; Boszormenyi-Nagy (1965) used the term "fusion" families wherein members experience themselves as an amorphous *we,* while Minuchin (1974) uses the term enmeshment.

Various researchers have offered different explanations as to how and why this occurs. Wynne noted that communication becomes blurred due to sudden shifts in focal attention, fragmentation, and vagueness in these families. Content of communication becomes sacrificed to avoid conflict that is seen as destructive of relationships. Bateson et al. (1956) felt that the patient is immobilized through double-binding communication. The verbal and nonverbal levels of communication are mutually contradictory, creating a no-win dilemma. They stress, as did Wynne, that this disqualifies the patient's perception and cognition, and thus prevents individuation. Some of these findings have been validated by the experimental laboratory studies of Reiss (1971). Reiss found the families of schizophrenic patients to be so "consensus sensitive" that they closed information input early to avoid differences, resulting in the poorest level of problem-solving as compared to families of delinquents and normals. Waxler (1974) also noted that schizophrenic youngsters solved problems better alone or when they were with normal families than when they were with their own family.

THE SYMBIOTIC SURVIVAL PATTERN

What makes the Symbiotic Survival Pattern different from these other formulations? First, it acknowledges the intrapsychic symbiotic fixation during childhood development of the patient. This is in keeping with psychoanalytic knowledge, although none of the previous theories in family therapy does this. Second, the Symbiotic Survival Pattern describes how the family interaction contributes to and then continues to reinforce this fixation in the patient. In schizophrenia, it also provides an explanation as to why object constancy does not occur, as well as why primary process thinking persists. The theory has also been extended to provide an understanding of family processes in depression, as well as in hysteria. Third, it was the first to use object-relations theory.

The Symbiotic Survival Pattern in Schizophrenia

The symbiotic fixation of the schizophrenic patient is not simply seen as due to intrapsychic fantasy during infancy—the actual form of relationship that exists in the family coincides with the kind of omnipotent, magical thinking that normally exists during the symbiotic phase of development. Thus the child's unconscious fantasy corresponds to the external reality in the family, contributing to fixation at this symbiotic phase. In these families, each member feels responsible for the self-esteem, identity, and survival of the other. Each family member feels controlled by his sense of responsibility for the self-esteem and survival of the other, and at the same time each needs to control the other's feelings, thoughts, and behavior. This produces a family power structure that is diffuse and encompassing, a system of pervasive mutual control with each member feeling both omnipotent and helpless at the same time. Since symbiotic binding involves control and disqualification of divergence in the patient's perception, thinking, feeling, and behavior, the greatest disruption occurs to ego functioning.

The Symbiotic Survival Pattern reinforces the child's egocentric, preoperational, primary process thinking. The child continues to feel in magical control over relationships instead of allowing the family to present an opposing reality essential for the development of secondary thought processes. Piaget (1954;1963) found that, during the preoperational period of development, children employed the concept of magical participation in the existence of external objects. Objects are seen as coming and going as a function of the child's physical action schema, wishes, or their sequence in time. Objects are not seen as having a separate and independent existence, but as surviving or not in response to the child's feelings, wishes, or behavior. The Symbiotic Survival Pattern reinforces this, and thus object constancy does not occur. Objects are not experienced as separate and stable, because the family system itself uses magical techniques to control relationships. The child remains pathologically dependent on the family. He feels he cannot survive alone nor can the family members survive without him. He needs to be sensitive to cues to control relationships.

The symbiotic form of relationship, even though it is pathogenic, becomes essential to the patient's functioning. The schizophrenic patient attempts to induce others into a symbiotic relationship, since it provides him with an identity that is reactive and relational to others and serves as a defense against destructive aggression. Laboratory experiments with schizophrenics validates the importance of symbiotic merging to sustain ego integrity (Silverman, 1975). Subliminal stimulation, using a tachistoscope, of symbiotic merging messages improved thought processes while aggressive messages diminished cognitive functioning.

How It Begins

The genesis of the Symbiotic Survival Pattern seems to stem from the developmental arrest in one or both parents, who relate to others as part objects and demonstrate fluid ego boundaries. The parents use the primitive defenses of projective-identification and splitting of the object into all good and all bad. Intrapsychic conflict of the parent is externalized, and the spouse and children unconsciously induced into acting out the conflict in the interpersonal sphere. In schizophrenia, scapegoating of the patient occurred when projective-identification of a bad self or bad parental image was put into the patient. When the good parental image was projected, the patient then served as a go-between or arbitrator between the parents and assumed responsibility for holding the family together. This latter type was more often found in female patients who were symbiotically bound to the father and manifested paranoid and hysteroid features. This latter type, with parentification of the patient, was described by Lidz in his schizmatic family.

Understanding Depressive Families

Our work with depressives and their families stems from two sources. The first was work with manic depressives by Cohen, et al (1954) and Fromm-Reichmann (1959), who noted these patients were pressured to achieve to enhance the prestige of the family. The second source was the work of Edith Jacobson (1971). She noted the child *intrapsychically* splits the parental object into a powerful, punitive parental image, that is incorporated in the superego, and a degraded, worthless parental image, incorporated in the "failing self-image." Jacobson postulates that, due to the child's *own* narcissistic idealization of himself, he sets up standards of achievement so high that he cannot live up to them, resulting in helplessness.

The Double-Bind over Achivement

It was determined that what Jacobson described was not simply limited to intrapsychic processes (Slipp, 1976). The actual family power structure was in reality a dominant-submissive one, with one parent powerful and punitive and the other weak and deflated. In their research, Lewis et al. (1976) also found this dominant-submissive family structure in families with a depressed patient. Here again, external reality corresponded to the child's intrapsychic fantasy. This congruence contributed to the reinforcement of the intrapsychic splitting of the parental object, instead of helping to integrate and resolve them. In addition, the pressure for achievement was actually exerted by the family, and not limited to intrapsychic idealization of the self. This pressure for achievement was exerted always by the dominant parent. It was overt, and this parent vicariously lived through the child's achievement to enhance his or her own self-esteem. The child internalized these goals, and they became part of his good, achieving self (S+, which Jacobson termed the wishful self-image). The child fears abandonment if he does not achieve these goals. At the same time, he feels responsible for the self-esteem of this parent, and remains dependent on this parent for his own self-worth.

Our work with families of depressives also noted that, even though this parent exploits the child for his or her own narcissistic enhancment with others, the child is *not gratified* when he does achieve. The achievement is never enough, it is taken for granted, or it is assumed that the next time the child will fail. Withholding gratification keeps the child weak, dependent, and under control. In addition, it covertly represents an unconscious message to *fail,* programming the child that he cannot win. To win, to be strong, and to be emancipated from control means to divest the dominant parent of power. The result is to invoke the wrath and jealousy of this dominant parent and to risk abandonment. The other parent in the family does provide nurturance for the child generally, but is submissive, depressed, and sees him or herself as a failure. The child is expected to compensate for this parent's failure; and thus to achieve further demeans this submissive parent. This also results in a threat of abandonment.

We have termed this family process in depression a *double-bind over achievement*. It is not as encompassing as the double-bind described in schizophrenia; it is limited to performance pressure, and thus involves the superego more than ego functioning. For the patient, this is a no-win dilemma; if he wins he loses, and if he loses he loses. We feel this entrapment is responsible for the *negative cognitive set,* for the patient's feelings of helplessness and hopelessness. The patient's social achievement only enhances the dominant parent's prestige; he is only a slave with nothing in it for himself. The result is that the patient feels exploited, demeaned, used, deprived, and enraged. Since the patient has not been prepared to function independently, the rage needs to be repressed. However, the rage can be expressed in several ways that are out of conscious awareness and will not destroy this dependent object relationship. One way is intrapsychically through *self-punishment.* Another way is interpersonally—the patient induces others through projective-identification to act out a repetition of the parental double-bind, but this time he frustrates their using him by self-defeating maneuvers.

Punishing and Inducing Punishment by Oppositional Symbiosis

The intrapsychic mechanism of self-punishment has been amply written about by Freud, Rado, Klein, Deutsch, Bibring, and Jacobson. Thus, only the interpersonal maneuver will be briefly described. The patient first induces others to expect some form of gratification from him, in terms of his performance in school, work, love, or in psychotherapy. The patient complies and then rebels against what he feels is demanded of him. He experiences himself as being externally pressured and dominated again. By passive-aggressive means he can frustrate the other's expectation of him through self-defeating acts, and thus defeat the other.

But this rebellion only goes so far to avoid rejection. He plays brinkmanship, always going to the edge. We have termed this relationship an *oppositional symbiosis*. The patient recreates a pathologically dependent situation where he feels dominated and pressured to perform. Then he can fight back to achieve an identity in reaction to the other. He is a counterpuncher, fighting against the demands of the dominant parental image for some autonomy. This represents a compromise solution to the original double-bind over achievement in his family of origin. The patient can thus rob the dominant parent of the spoils of his success, and, in addition, by having complied to the fail message and been masochistically self-defeating, he can feel *entitled* to demand love and support.

To summarize, the depressive recreates the internalized object relations from childhood in the interpersonal field by inducing others to act out internal mental images. The depressive personality externalizes the dominant parental image. During the depressive episode, the dominant parental image in the superego punishes the bad self-image in the ego. In mania, the bad, failing self-image is projected into another, who is demeaned and punished while the patient identifies with the dominant parental image himself. Arieti (1962) has described how the depressive views himself as worthless, while transfering onto others the image of the "dominant other." Jacobson (1971) also discusses this, even pointing out that in paranoid conditions *both* the punitive, dominant parental image and the failing, bad self-image may be externalized. She reports a case where the patient induced a boy to act out so as to live vicariously through the boy's bad behavior. At the same time, the patient sent and paid for the boy's therapy. Finally, the patient betrayed the boy by informing his therapist and parents of the boy's bad conduct so that they would punish the boy. Thus, both the bad self and punitive parental image were externalized simultaneously, instead of just one, or flip-flopping back and forth between them as often is the case.

Hysteria: The Patient as "Go-between"

In hysteria, the family seems to contain some structures found in the families of *both* schizophrenic and depressive patients (Slipp, 1977).

1. The patient was involved in a Symbiotic Survival Pattern, and placed in the role of "go-between."
2. Maternal deprivation and underprotection occurred, with the daughters needing to find mother surrogates.
3. A dominant-submissive power structure exists as in depressive and obsessive families.
4. A collusion of silence exists about certain areas; however, physical illness is responded to with concern.
5. The fathers were narcissistic, often alcoholic or sociopathic, and the symbiotic binding took the form of *seduction*. We found that the more the daughter could identify with the dominant, seductive father, the greater the chance for development of a neurotic hysterical personality. If the daughter is first seductively bound and then betrayed and rejected, the daughter is then thrown onto identifying with the victimized mother. The tendency here is for the development of a borderline (hysteroid) personality with depressive and paranoid features.

Varieties of Symbiotic Binding

In 1931, Freud published "Libidinal Types" a paper in which he attempted to differentiate which individuals were prone to develop certain neuroses. He speculated there was an inborn distribution of libidinal energy. The narcissistic type, prone to psychosis and criminality, was under the supremacy of the ego; while the obsessional was under the superego; and the erotic type, tending to develop hysteria, was under the id. Instead of viewing these as purely intrapsychic and genetic, I consider them as related to the type of symbiotic binding occuring in the family. Symbiotic binding primarily influences the ego in schizophrenia, the superego in obsessive-depressive disorders, and the id in hysteria. Thus, a typology of family interaction characteristic of each of these disorders, as well as which aspect of the personality structure most affected, is suggested. Not only is this typology useful in establishing a diagnosis, but it has immediate value in the treatment of families or individuals. One can be sensitized to the occurrences of certain patterns of family interaction that are pathogenic, instead of discounting them as distortions of the patient. These patterns, stemming from the family of origin, are acted out in the marital family, as well as with the therapist.

Application to Individual Treatment

A case illustration will be helpful in demonstrating how the Symbiotic Survival Pattern can be useful in treatment. Since knowledge of family dynamics can also be helpful in individual treatment, the case of a depressed patient reported in my paper, "An Intrapsychic-Interpersonal Theory of Depression" (1976) will be presented.

The patient was a talented writer who came for psychoanalysis because of symptoms of depression, work inhibition, and marital conflict. Despite a promising beginning to his career, he felt immobilized and unable to concentrate on his writing. This resulted in financial hardships, insecurity, and conflict with his wife. In this case, the succeed-fail double-bind came not only from the father, but also existed between the parents.

His father was depicted as overtly dominant, cold, and overfunctional. Father had wanted to become a physician but, because of the Depression, settled for teaching. Despite his eventually becoming a school principal, father felt dissatisfied with his achievement, and saw himself as a failure. He pressured his son (the patient) into academic and athletic achievement. This was particularly intense when his son was a student in his school.

The patient felt his father was solely interested in "the appurtenances of success" for his own prestige, and not genuinely interested in him. At the same time, the patient felt his father was competitive with him; as he stated, "I had to prove my inability to cope, to be inadequate, and I have to do something to pull myself down. Whenever I have a creative good idea, I have to pay dues first. To you, to my father. I was to have the rewards of society—be famous, rich, and successful—so he could show me off. But somewhere he didn't really want me to be truly potent. He had to put me down. I would expose him if I were adequate, he had put himself down by settling for something he didn't want to do. He was always paying dues. I pay dues to be a little potent, I play brinkmanship. I kill myself and him just a little bit—I never have a full heart on, only half a heart to preserve the relationship."

His being a loser thus served to comply with father's fail message, as well as being an expression of the patient's rebellion at being exploited by his father for his own self-esteem needs. Thus, he could frustrate father's pressure for achievement without being held accountable. He was fearful of directly asserting himself with his father because of considerable castration anxiety. He introjected his threatening father (in his superego). In his dreams, either he saw himself as a wolf going for his father's jugular or else being killed by him. He was fearful of his father's power and of his own omnipotent rage, and wanted to be controlled. He identified with his submissive and depressed mother (which became part of his self-image). In one of his dreams, he promised his father that he would behave like a good girl. "The only way I could assert myself with father was by being passive. It was the only weapon I had, the only way to express anger." When his father depended on him for performance, the patient felt protected against his power, although at the same time he felt deprived, trapped, and enraged. "There was an element of *spite* in my losing, but it was the only way I could get back."

He felt guilty over letting his father down, and projected his guilt and self-hatred onto me in the transference. He felt I would be like his introjected father—disappointed, judgmental, and angry. He thereby externalized his self-punishing intrapsychic maneuver (the bad parental image punishing the bad self-image) to expiate his guilt and turn the bad parental introject into the good one, which could then reunite with the good self-image. He could thus sustain his oppositional symbiotic relationship, achieve some autonomy, control his own rage, control his father's responses, as well as express his anger indirectly without being held accountable.

Mother was described as submissive to father, underfunctional, and warm to the patient. She had been her mother's favorite, infantilized, and remained dependently attached. When she married, she and her husband moved into her parents' home and lived with them for about nine years. She and her mother formed an alliance against her husband, putting down his education as useless, since he could not earn a living (during the Depression). The patient's mother had dropped out of high school, since education and intellectuality were not valued in her home. The patient described his mother as neurasthenic; she suffered from headaches, insomnia, feelings of worthlessness and helplessness, and hypochondriasis. She instilled anxiety in the patient concerning his own bodily functions, as well as a constricted, negative world outlook. She had no confidence in herself to achieve, and saw her son as similar to herself. She never expected anything from the patient and took no interest in his performance. When the family moved out of his grandparents' house, his mother formed a seductive alliance with him, treating him as an intimate and complaining about father's stinginess with money. The patient felt "at the mercy of her ignorance" and controlled by her weakness. She was in a constant state of dysphoria, but never did anything for herself.

The patient felt his mother needed his reassurance, and he felt responsible for her sense of adequacy and happiness. (He assumed the role of *savior* in this symbiotic relationship.) The patient stated, "I was in some way responsible for how both my parents felt. My station was making it up to them. I had no right to my independence or to good times, if they were miserable. My parents were both weak and unable to function as separate people. I always took my cues from them also to define myself . . . I always felt like a helpless child who couldn't cope. I remained dependent on others. I felt I had to perform to be loved, otherwise I'd be abandoned. My father would never say you're doing well or I don't care how you do, I love you . . . It was always connected with making good for him. I don't want to give anything to anyone except my children."

The patient then worked through his relationship with his wife, who had been seen also as a bad, exploitative (dominant) parent. Any expectation at all was interpreted as an unfair demand; he resented it and withheld gratification just enough to avoid rejection. As the patient worked through his conflicts with his parents in the transference, he became productive and successful as a writer, as well as financially secure. The relationship with his wife improved as he became more giving and supportive of her needs.

Selecting Family Therapy Strategies

Divergent strategies or approaches in family therapy appear to produce change. The Symbiotic Survival Pattern will be used to provide a theoretical basis for understanding this paradox. To begin with, in family therapy, perhaps more than any other form of psychological treatment, there is keen sensitivity to *covert* messages expressed between people. Freud's recognition of the importance of symptomatic acts in *Psychopathology of Everyday Life* introduced the use of nonverbal cues to the understanding of unconscious dynamics. For example, when nonverbal elements contradicted verbal communication, this was brought to the attention of the patient. However, it was not until the work of Bateson et al. (1956) on the double-bind, that the pathogenic significance of covert messages was suggested. The patient was trapped in a no-win dilemma that was felt to contribute to the development of schizophrenia. Here the verbal, overt message was contradicted by the nonverbal, covert message. Our understanding of nonverbal, covert messages was extended by the work of Scheflen (1963) in kinesics. Scheflen pointed out how nonverbal bodily and facial cues were used to monitor behavior and revealed power relationships in the family.

What the Symbiotic Survival Pattern points out is that nonverbal, *covert* communication is the major pathway for *projective-identification* to induce another person into a role. These roles differ with various disorders and are determined by the particular split introjected image of self or parent. The theory also differentiates double-binding communication. In schizophrenia, it encompasses perception, cognition, feelings, and behavior;while in depression it is more limited to performance of goals related to achievement.

If we look at the techniques in family therapy to provide change, we note that, in the psychoanalytic approach, the emphasis is on making covert communication and patterns overt— the major tool is through the use of verbal insight, to understand intellectually and to work through emotions; change comes from cognitive restructuring and release of emotions, and is a process coming from *within* the individual. In the structural and strategic approaches in family therapy, understanding of genetic factors is bypassed, while the here-and-now is emphasized; leverage for change comes through the therapists use of covert communication to manipulate the system of interaction—here change comes from *outside* and affects the individuals in the family.

In strategic family therapy, Selvini-Pallazoli (1978) uses the very technique that induced the patient to be symptomatic, the double-bind. However, she does not use it to exploit the patient for one's own personality needs, as was the case originally, but for therapeutic purposes. The therapist gives the family a verbal prescription that overtly goes along with the symptom, and thus the family homeostasis is not threatened and resistances aroused. On a covert level, however, the patient is really expected to change. For example, a depressive might be told to continue failing socially, since by failing he is really protecting his father's self-esteem, and thus helping the family. The secondary gain of the symptom, that was formerly covert, is now openly brought to conscious awareness, which makes it difficult to continue with the symptom. The meaning of the symptom in terms of the family relationships is now exposed. Thus, a covert message is given in this therapeutic double-bind expecting change. In this clever maneuver, the therapist cannot lose, nor the patient, one hopes. In a personal communication with Selvini-Pallazoli, she informed me that, although change often does occur, the therapist becomes an object of resentment. I would interpret this as due to the therapist assuming the role of the dominant, punitive parent, which stimulates the development of a negative parental transference. Thus, the patient's opposition and spitefulness is harnessed in the service of health.

Minuchin, in his structural approach, similarly attempts to change family interaction that supports the patient's symptomatic behavior by manipulating the covert level of communication. Minuchin restricts himself to a phenomenological level, describing interaction without developing a theoretical system to explain why this occurs. He borrows from Lidz's concepts of generational boundaries and Wynne's pseudomutuality. Although Minuchin does not use the labels of the Symbiotic Survival Pattern, he is aware that the patient assumes the roles of scapegoat, go-between, and savior to preserve family relationships, of symbiotic relatedness, which he terms enmeshment, as well as power relations. He employs nonverbal, covert behavior to change the power structure of the family. He controls communication patterns by including or excluding members, even changing seating arrangements deliberately. He backs the weaker parent and weakens the dominant parent. He reinforces the sibling subsystem. In those ways, he changes the power structure sufficiently, to enable the patient to have the strength to emerge from the projective-identification image that has been imposed on him, and to strive for a separate identity. Minuchin also relabels conflict as beneficial and harmony as a lack of relatedness. Thus, he attacks the covert family role that conflict is dangerous and destructive to relationships. If conflict can be brought to an overt level and discussed by the parents, the need for splitting and projective-identification by them will be diminished. As they are able to integrate their ambivalent feelings and work through conflict, the need to induce the patient into a particular role is eliminated. Thus, change can occur.

Murray Bowen's systems approach is perhaps closest to the psychoanalytic in family therapy. He stresses generational transmission of patterns; thus, genetic factors are emphasized. By having the spouses actually visit with and change their relationships in their families of origin, the reenactment of transferential distortions may be eliminated. Bowen also stresses the use of "I" language in family therapy. My reasons for doing so are as follows: The use of "they" tends to reinforce generalizations and to deny personal responsibility. "We" does not differentiate the individual, but bolsters symbiotic relatedness. "You" language tends to foster projection of unacceptable aspects of the self onto another, particularly scapegoating. Perhaps Bowen's most significant contribution theoretically has been the importance of triangular relationships, particularly in families who are poorly differentiated.

The Symbiotic Survival Pattern has also stressed the importance of triadic relationships in schizophrenia, depression, and hysteria; however, the triadic nature of these relationships is explained through object-relations theory. Due to the pre-oedipal level of personality organization in the parents, splitting and projective-identification of part-object images remain significant. An aspect of either the good or bad self or parental image is put into two family members simultaneously through projective-identification. Because of the fluid ego boundaries between individuals, these are incorporated and acted out interpersonally to create maladaptive patterns of interaction. For example, in families of the hysteric, the spouse may be seen as the bad parent while the patient is induced into acting out the good parental image, thereby playing the role of go-between in the family. In schizophrenia, when scapegoating of the patient occurs, projection of the bad self or bad parental image into the patient occurs while simultaneously the spouse is maintained as the idealized good parent. In depression, the patient is expected to be the family savior by enacting the good self-image while the spouse is demeaned and punished as the bad self-image, the failure.

It is interesting that psychoanalysis has been most successful in treating neurotic disorders. Perhaps this is so because the very technique evokes dyadic relationships. In neurosis, the fixation is oedipal, and there has been an integration of split introjects. Ego boundaries are more definitive and there is projection of ambivalence, with both positive and negative feelings towards the same individual. The dyadic relationship changes to include other individuals at different times during the treatment, but with the neurotic it remains dyadic generally. The technique of family therapy arose in the setting of treating sicker families, initially schizophrenics and their families. Here triadic relationships are more significant because of splitting and simultaneous projective-identification of two introjects into two individuals. Triadic transference-countertransference interactions exist in these families. The very addition of a therapist to a marital couple or a family itself also tends to evoke a triadic transferential reaction. Thus, it is not surprising that family therapy has been so useful in the treatment of sicker families where triadic relationships are so important.

Using the Symbiotic Survival Pattern in Psychoanalytic Family Therapy

Use and awareness of the Symbiotic Survival Pattern is helpful in understanding and conducting psychoanalytic family treatment. A collaborative and more equal type of relationship is fostered, where the patients can form a therapeutic alliance with the therapist. Insight into maladaptive patterns is achieved in a climate of trust and mutual respect. Transferential patterns of a triadic nature can be interpreted, so that integration of splitting and working through of ambivalence can occur. Interpretations are always made in a nonthreatening, nondomineering manner, but in a manner that understands and accepts the context of why certain events needed to be expressed the way they were. This understanding and respect leads to self-respect and efforts to change maladaptive interaction. The all good or all bad type of thinking manifested by splitting may give way to alternative ways of thinking and behaving. The Symbiotic Survival Pattern may serve to sensitize the therapist to three major areas in the treatment of the family. These areas are selection, shaping, and countertransference. I shall discuss each one briefly.

SELECTION

Mate selection by each spouse occurs through the unconscious recognition that the other individual has features that fit one's own internalized object relations. An empathic link is established as each unconsciously perceives a complementary fit of internalized mental representations. This fit enables projective-identification of mental images to occur more easily, so that maladaptive patterns can be reestablished. The spouses are usually at the same developmental level. It takes two to play the game.

SHAPING

With the development of conflict in the marriage, certain roles will be evoked through projective-identification which involve the simultaneous projection of partial-object representations onto two individuals. These roles and mental images vary with the type of disorder that evolves, as mentioned above.

COUNTERTRANSFERENCE

To connote the newer, broader definition of countertransference as developed by Racker (1957) and Kernberg (1975), this term is not restricted to the older meaning of representing the analyst's own neurotic reactions from his own past that are projected onto the patient—instead, it also describes the responses of the therapist to the patient's attempts to make him or her feel or behave certain ways through projective identification. This force is particularly potent in family therapy, and no matter what the approach, all family therapists are alert not to be sucked into the family system. It is important for the therapist to be aware of his own feelings and not to be induced into behaving in a way that corresponds to the image placed into him through projective-identification. To do so only reinforces maladaptive family patterns and prevents their recognition and resolution.

REFERENCES

Arieti, S. The Psychotherapeutic Approach to Depression. *American Journal of Psychotherapy.* 1962, *16,* 397–406.
Bateson, F., Jackson, D. D., Haley, J., & Weakland, J. H. Toward a Theory of Schizophrenia. *Behavioral Science,* 1956, *1,* 251–264.
Boszormenyi-Nagy, I. A theory of relationships: Experience and transaction *In* Boszormenyi-Nagy, I., & Framo, J. L. (Eds.). Intensive family therapy. New York: Hoeber Medical Division, Harper and Row, 1965.
Bowen, M. Family concept of schizophrenia. In Jackson, D. D. (Ed.). Etiology of schizophrenia. New York: Basic Books, 1960.
Cohen, M. B., Baker, G., Cohen, R. A., et al. An Intensive Study of Twelve Cases of Manic Depressive Psychosis. *Psychiatry,* 1954, *17,* 103–138.
Freud, S. Libidinal types. Collected Papers 5. London: Hogarth, (1931) 1952.
Fromm-Reichmann, F. Psychoanalysis and psychotherapy. Selected Papers. Chicago: University of Chicago, 1959.
Jacobson, E. Psychotic conflict and reality. New York: International University, 1967.
Jacobson, E. Depression: Comparative studies of normal, neurotic, and psychotic conditions. New York: International University, 1971.
Kernberg, O. Borderline conditions and pathological narcissism. New York: Aronson, 1975.

Levinson, D. Role, personality and social structure. *In* Coser, L. A., & Rosenberg, B. (Eds.). Sociological theory: A book of readings. New York: MacMillan, 1964.

Lewis, J. M., Beavers, W. R., Gossett, J. T., & Phillips, V. A. No single thread: Psychological health in family systems. New York: Brunner Mazel, 1976.

Lidz, T., Fleck, S., and Cornelison, A. R. Schizophrenia and the family. New York: International University, 1965.

Mahler, M. S., & Furer, M. On human symbiosis and the vicissitudes of individuation. volume 1. New York, International University, 1968.

Minuchin, S. Families and family therapy. Cambridge, Harvard University Press, 1974.

Piaget, J. The construction of reality in the child. New York: Basic Books, 1954.

Piaget, J. Realism and the origin of the idea of participation. *In* The child's conception of the world. Patterson, N.J.: Littlefield Adams, 1963, pp. 123–136.

Racker, H. The meaning and Uses of Countertransference. *Psychoanalytic Quarterly,* 1957, *26,* 303–357.

Reiss, D. Varieties of Consensual Experience. III. Contrasts between Families of Normals, Delinquents, and Schizophrenics. *Journal of Nervous and Mental Disease,* 1971, *152,* 73–95.

Scheflen, A. Communication and Regulation in Psychotherapy. *Psychiatry,* 1963, *2,* 126–136.

Selvini-Palazzoli, M. et al. Paradox and counterparadox. New York: Aronson, 1978.

Silverman, L.H., Levinson, P., Mendelsohn, E., Ungaro, R., & Bernstein, A. A Clinical Application of Subliminal Psychodynamic Activation: On the Stimulation of Symbiotic Fantasies as an Adjunct in the Treatment of Hospitalized Schizophrenics. *Journal of Nervous and Mental Disease,* 1975, *161,* 379–392.

Slipp, S. The Symbiotic Survival Pattern: A Relational Theory of Schizophrenia. *Family Process,* 1973, *12,* 377–398.

Slipp, S. An Intrapsychic-Interpersonal Theory of Depression. *Journal of the American Academy of Psychoanalysis,* 1976, *4,* 389–409.

Slipp, S. Interpersonal Factors in Hysteria: Freud's Seduction Theory and The Case of Dora. *Journal of American Academy of Psychoanalysis,* 1977, *5,* 359–376.

Waxler, N. E. Parent and Child Effects on Cognitive Performance: An Experimental Approach to The Etiological and Responsive Theories of Schizophrenia. *Family Process,* 1974, *13,* 1–22.

Wynne, L. G., Ryckoff, I. M., Day, J., & Hirsch, S. Pseudomutuality in The Family Relations of Schizophrenics. *Psychiatry* 1958, *21,* 205–220.

David Kantor, Ph.D.

9
Critical Identity Image:
A Concept Linking Individual,
Couple, and Family Development

Minuchin and other structural family therapists have indicated
the importance of crisis in family therapy. Distinguishing between "emergencies" and "crisis," Minuchin has convincingly
demonstrated that a period of crisis can be the start of lasting
changes: As family therapists, we often induce and use crises. We
intervene by producing unstable situations that require change
and the restructuring of family organizations. Indeed, heavy reliance on system crises by him and other structuralists makes
crisis, both system-made and therapeutically induced, the virtual
trademark of structural therapy.

I see a crisis as a temporary breakdown of structural laws
governing a system. In itself, a crisis is a normal occurrence in a
family system. Indeed, the resolution of crises is the basis for the
formation of new structures, and crises are, therefore, an integral
part of development. From this perspective we can understand
development in a family system to be a series of changes or transformations in the system's structure, changes that are the end
product of resolutions of the crises. But what do we really know
about system development?

Family system development has not received the attention it
deserves from family theorists and therapists. One obvious reason

for this (though not the only one) is the subject's complexity. Systems are multidimensional. Which of their dimensions, then, are we to chart? Family systems can be viewed at different levels. Do we study all the levels, all the subsystems, including individuals and *their* subsystems? These questions are the framework in which I organize my thoughts about system development and, through its key concept, *critical identity image,* link individual and system phenomena. I will elaborate this developmental framework, discuss some clinical implications of the concept, and, finally, offer a clinical application.

A DEVELOPMENTAL FRAMEWORK

Systems therapists have traditionally ignored intrapsychic contents, because systems theory is more concerned with formal structures, i.e., with patterns of behaviors. Contents involve memories and their inner meanings (which are not observable) and themes and the relationships between themes (which are related to history and, therefore, linear rather than circular propositions about causality). Systems theorists prefer circular causality, feedback loops.

A family developmental theory cannot do without contents or without history. I start with the assumption that families must be understood in terms of both formal (transactional) structures and content structures, and that an understanding of both and how they come together is essential in all therapy, but especially in couples and family therapy.

Levels of Organization

This framework distinguishes four levels of system organization. Family system development is development on all four levels. This is not a time framework, like Erikson's epigenetic framework; it is a hierarchy of increasing levels of complexity.

1. The level of *meaning structures* is the family's foundation— the personal meanings each individual brings to and acquires in the system: their histories, myths and lores, icons or symbols, the things they notice and talk about.

2. The level of *action structures* is the family's behavioral repertoire, the raw doings. When the dog barks to get out, it's let
   out. That is an action structure.
3. The pattern level of organization, *strategic structures,* consists of the family's characteristic strategies and sequences.
   For example, anyone in the family can walk the dog, but
   when I come down in the morning and find dog excrement on
   the rug, I cannot directly complain to the dog's owner, my
   stepdaughter, but must complain to my wife who, with un-
   complicated directness, tells her daughter to clean it up.
4. The highest level of organization, the family's *model structures,* is drawn from elements of the three lower levels to form
   ideals, the system's ideals and goals, that jointly define the
   family's *core purpose.* For example, we might say, "In our
   family we really appreciate each other." The statement
   exemplifies part of the core purpose. These ideals also include
   the preferred ways of regulating conflicts, for example, "We
   do not shrink from facing our disagreements in a good fight!"

EMPIRICAL CONCEPTS IN THE CONTEXT OF CRISIS

When you see a family, you don't see the model structure or
the meaning structure. These are conceptual entities, reifica-
tions. You see the action and the patterns of action. Corresponding to the four levels of organization (Model, Pattern, Action, and
Meaning Structures), there are four levels of empirical concepts
(Fig. 1). In a crisis, you *see* the breakdown of two of them, *steering
mechanisms* and *psychopolitics.*

Steering Mechanisms

Steering mechanisms are patterns of actions. Every living
system develops mechanisms as a means of reaching its goals. A
family's mechanisms, therefore, are like the "plays" or
"strategies" a football team uses to score, make goals and, on the
good days, win its games. Steering mechanisms are a special subset of mechanisms (see chapter 5, 6, 7 of *Inside the Family*): the
ones family systems specially develop for, and then call upon, in

	General Levels of Organization	Equivalent Empirical Concepts	Crisis Constructs
IV.	Model Structure	Collective Identity	Model "Instability"
III.	Pattern Structure	Steering Mechanisms	Mechanism "Breakdown"
II.	Action Structure	Four Player Model of System Psychopolitics	"Stuck" Psychopolitics
I.	Meaning Structure	Critical Identity Image	"Competing" Identity Claims

Increasing Conceptual Complexity and Richness
(Substantive)

Content Structures

Formal Structures (vertical axis label)

Fig. 1.   A family system developmental framework.

crisis situations. When obstacles from the outside interfere with a system's routine capacities for reaching its goals, or when competition over the definitions of goals or the means of reaching them, develops from within, the system calls upon its steering mechanisms. In short, steering mechanisms are a family's decision-making, problem-solving, crisis-resolving plays or strategies.

During a developmental crisis, the family system's steering mechanisms break down. Before this breakdown occurs, there are moments of opportunity when the family has a chance either to come up with one of its clutch strategies or to forge a new one for the occasion. When they do neither, the crisis escalates. The escalation is not a passive happening but requires active cooperation and collusion. Think of the football team that is one touchdown behind its opponent near the end of the game and is facing a third-and-seven situation deep in its own territory. Should the team fail to select and execute a play that allows it to keep the ball and make the down, it's likely to lose the game. The team's huddle, a structure built into the game of football (at least originally) for assessing one's own and one's opponent's strengths and weaknesses and selecting both the play and the individual player assignments, is a structural analogy to the behavior of the family in moments of opportunity and decision when a family crisis process can go either way. Failure to cooperate in order to design and execute the clutch strategy in the football game is functionally equivalent to a breakdown in the family system's steering mechanisms.

Psychopolitics

Psychopolitics refers to an individual's acts and actions in relation to others in the system. The Four Player Model of system psychopolitics is the concept I use for denoting and analyzing observable system behaviors. In this model, people who are interacting with one another in any interpersonal context have four and only four "parts" to play: mover, follower, opposer and bystander. A *mover* is one who defines or initiates an action. A *follower* agrees with, supports, or continues the action. An *opposer* challenges or goes against the actions. A *bystander* witnesses an action, but remains outside, acknowledging neither agreement nor disagreement, sometimes in an active way. Preferences for particular positions derive, in part, from biological or psychological predisposition, but the primary source of a player's action repertoire is the family and other institutional experiences in which individuals learn what parts they are allowed or required to play in specific transactions and contexts. "Preferences" are established when individual predisposition and family rules settle into stable action structures.

A system's psychopolitical configuration is like its signature. For example, one family develops a feisty style (a prevalence of mover-opposer behaviors), another a peaceful style (a prevalence of mover-follower behaviors), and another an intellectual style (a prevalence of mover-bystander behaviors). Such decisively differentiated styles are not "pathological" in themselves. The question is always, how well does the style work? Are the family members satisfied? Does the community object? (If it does, it will eventually make its disapproval felt.)

Although there are typical preferences, for a system to function efficiently, all four psychopolitical parts are necessary. A system without movers is dull; a system without followers can't reach its goals; a system without opposers learns nothing new from within; and a system without bystanders is more likely to get stuck in the repetition of unsuccessful strategies. Indeed, the degree of flexibility in psychopolitical behavior is an important general index of a system's functioning. As a rule, the most "well-functioning" system is one that permits all players a high degree of freedom in playing all parts in all of the system's transactional contexts; that is, each person is, at least on occasion, a mover, a follower, an opposer, or a bystander.

In specific crisis contexts, psychopolitical behavior becomes stuck. A "stuck" player is a player who, in the same context, always operates in only one of the four player positions. An example: the father who keeps choosing the college his son is to be allowed to attend, finds every time that the particular college he picked is unacceptable to his son: both mover and opposer are stuck. During crisis, rigid stereotyping tends to replace whatever flexibility has been established for noncrisis situations. The crisis "escalation" may be the escalation of blind obedience or mutual withdrawal.

Turning again to our football analogy: Imagine the handicap to the team if, on returning to his huddle, the end could not report that his opposing end is limping and, therefore, advocate an "end around" play. In his inability to initiate, he would be a disabled mover. If the quarterback wouldn't use information relayed from the stadium-top spotter, passed down to coach to team via a substitution, then the spotter's bystanding function would be disabled. If the players could not oppose the proposal of the absentminded quarterback to repeat a disastrous pass play (that had always led to interceptions by that particular rival team), then the opposing function would be disabled. If the halfback refused or merely didn't execute his usual block, would we be harsh to call him a disabled follower? We think not!

A *ritualized developmental crisis* occurs when family members take highly predictable, self-defeating, system-disabling player positions at critical moments in the crisis cycle. An example: The father who kept choosing his son's college not only makes the first move, but does so in a way that is certain, absolute, and conveys to the family that if his son does not obey, something terrible will happen. In this setting, his wife, filled with despair that they (father and son) never seem to get along, remains silent, which doubly incenses the son. He is outraged at his father's predictable dogmatism, and is dismayed at his mother's silence. They may shift to different disabled player behaviors at different stages in the crisis. At a later stage in the above-mentioned crisis, the mother may move to lukewarmly support her husband, which may then drive the son to violence.

Moreover, the "stuckness" of key persons' moves and patterns of moves during the *ritual impasse* serves to limit or destroy the options other members have for suggesting strategies for coping with the crisis or for seeking resolutions. Since it seems that neither father nor son will listen to mother's suggestions of alternative ways of picking a school during the crisis, she sees no alternative to silence, except when, as her son behaves increasingly outrageously, she feels she must side with father. This is the "stuck following" that in this family leads to violence.

COLLECTIVE IDENTITY—THREE FAMILY STYLES

What makes a family dynamic is that each of the members has ideas about what the family is to *be* and *become*. These ideas are often in conflict. The collective identity is the total set of those ideas and whatever consensus can be managed at any particular time. With time these ideas develop, and lead to impasses that lead to crises that require new ideas. Thus, a family collective identity is usually changing through time and is transformed through crises.

My previous empirical research suggested that family styles could be usefully sorted into three groups: closed, open, and random. I think that collective identities can be similarly sorted. Of course, we know that families are enormously variable, and there's room for argument about how best to sort them; but, I will discuss that variability only in terms of the three groups, or models.

Three Family Styles

My classification schema identifies three models: closed, open, and random. While every family typically evolves a unique configuration of patterns, strategies, and rules, often blending characteristics of each pure type, most families tend toward one or another of the three forms. All three are "good" and "workable" models. Each has its own successful and unsuccessful variety.

The three models differ in three important ways:

1. Each model defines its *core purpose* differently: The closed style seeks *stability* and relies on the certainties of *tradition.* The open espouses *adaptation,* which it arrives at through dialectic and consensus. The random prefers *exploration* with a reliance on *intuition.*

2. Each model has a different homeostatic ideal: The closed system relies on negative feedback or constancy maintaining loops; e.g., only strict conformity to traditional norms is rewarded, and as happens more often, signs of deviance are punished. The open system stresses a balance between negative and positive feedback; e.g., deviance is punished, but initiative toward novelty may be rewarded. The random system relies on positive feedback or variety stimulating loops; e.g., novelty is encouraged.

3. Each model defines the goals within the major dimensions of family life with different words. Of course, for families of all three models the goals of the dimensions *affect, power,* and *meaning* are really the same. The goals of affect are *nurturance* and a sense of *intimacy;* of power, a sense of *efficacy* and *competency;* of meaning, *validation* and a sense of *belonging.* But each model sees these dimensions, defines their goals, and governs activity within them in different ways, according to the core purpose and homeostatic ideals.

    In the closed model: Meaning is generated and perpetuated through reliance on rationality, tradition, and traditional symbols. Affect is characterized by earnest and sincere emotions and control of public demonstrations of emotion. Strong loyalty to the family is characteristic. Power is organized vertically, rules are clear, and opposition is discouraged.

    In the open model: Meaning emerges from the consideration of different points of view and the process of dialectic argument. Uniquely personal values and meanings are expressed and authenticity is expected. Affect is expressed openly and shared rather than withheld. Dissent can be voiced or even encouraged, but loyalty to both the family's individualistic and collectivistic ideals is still expected. Power is lateral and universal participation is expected.

In the random model: Meaning and reasoning tend to be dominated by personal inspiration; paradox and ambiguity are preferred modes of expression. Affect tends to be passionate, rapt, and quick. Power is also determined more experimentally than in the other models, and charisma and personal ability prevail. The random style is extravagant in paying tribute to potentiality.

When individual's models are in disagreement, model instability exists. Most families will show model instability in some dimensions. For example, A family might have no model instability in the meaning sphere, (where everyone agrees on values, modes of expressing ideas, or on what is proper public conduct) yet disagree in the power sphere as to the types of constraints to impose on violations of proper conduct or in the manner for deciding who in the family is better able to acquire resources from the outside world. On the more formal level, a developmental crisis precipitates the retesting of the family's core purpose as well as its homeostatic ideal, that is, its preferred means for controlling and regulating deviance. A family in which the mother's preferred style is random and the father's closed, might experience a crisis when their son brings home a bad conduct report from the school. The parents, because they operate with different core purposes (based on different critical identity images) and different homeostatic ideals suggestive of different ways for regulating deviance, will respond to the event in different ways. These differences or model instabilities, can become the source of new system structures, new rules and strategies, if the struggle over models gets resolved.

This resolution can occur in one of several ways:

1. The source of the instability can be externalized. In the example, the parents might blame the school for hiring inadequate staff, and in so doing avoid the internal conflict between their operating models.

2.   They could resolve the instability through incorporating a
     new rule, which, for example, assigned to the mother the task
     of making periodic contact with the school so that the father
     is not surprised by reports. Here, they cooperate in working
     out assigned roles that do not violate either's preferred
     model.
3.   No resolution, in which case the system becomes immobilized
     and the model instability remains fixed in dysfunctional
     rules and structures. Here, the family becomes disabled in
     reaching these particular goals for its members, and the
     model instabilities can become a chronic source of family ten-
     sion that erupts each time a new event sets off the same basic
     structural problem.

HYPOTHESIS

*A normal developmental crisis is an identity struggle taking
place on all four system levels.* The more outward features of the
crisis are: (1) a temporary collapse of the system's problem-
solving capabilities, that is, a breakdown in its *steering
mechanisms* (events occuring at the pattern level of organization); and, (2) a constriction and rigidification of its behavior (at
the action level of organization), that is, a gravitation into stuck
psychopolitics. Less visible features of the crisis are on the meaning and model levels. The struggle begins at the least complex
level of organization, the meaning level, where it is fueled by
competing critical identity images, and continues through to the
most complex level, the model level, where model instabilities
based on competing ideals for the shaping of a collective identity
might potentially be resolved. Crisis, therefore, equals identity
struggle. A family developmental crisis occurs when the family
system is temporarily immobilized by competing identity claims.

While unresolved identity crises can result in divorce (emotional or legal), the resolution of identity crises are responsible for
two kinds of developmental changes: (1) the acquisition of new
structures and an increase in structural complexity and efficiency
as system members clarify their rules, evolve strategies for more
expediently reaching their goals, and clarify and perfect their
model for living; and (2) the gradual increase in conceptual com-

plexity and the gradual enrichment of communicational life as the private symbols, images and themes of individual members, clash and complement, remain at impasse, and/or are set aside or creatively synthesize in a richer and more broadly sustaining collective identity.

THE RITUAL IMPASSE: THE IMAGISTIC REPRESENTATION OF CRISIS

The ritual impasse—a term I use for recurrent, episodic playing out of the family identity crisis—is of key clinical importance. The ritual impasse can be a ridiculously wasteful, utterly destructive exercise in mutually induced despair. In the ritual impasse, family members demarcate their boundaries and assert their separate realities. Polarization is the typical outcome, and alienation the typical aftermath. But the ritual impasse is also a positive assertion and representation of identity, an opportunity for transformation, a scenario for family development. Generational and transgenerational aspects of the ritual are also important. The ritual impasse involves an assertion by the individuals involved that their inner meanings are not to be ignored and that they see themselves as transmitters of legitimate ideal values.

Introducing the Concept "Image"

The link between the formal structures a family develops over its life cycle and the content that is the foundation of communicational life, both behavioral and symbolic, is the image. Image is an organism's subjective knowledge structure, what it *believes* to be true. We can speak of an individual's image or of a family's image. We can speak of the image possessed by an organism, implying something general and holistic about its knowledge structure; or we can speak of an image among several, implying that individuals and family systems develop separate images for different purposes. Indeed, each family evolves out of the interaction and eventual collectivization of the identity images each of the adults brings into the marriage relationship.

DEFINITION OF "IMAGE"

Images are internalized memory pictures. One can think of them as pictorialized representations of events, as thoughts in visual form, or as pictorialized thought schemas, depending upon how one wishes to distribute emphasis of the sensory and cognitive elements that they contain. It seems to me best to view the image as an integration of sensibility and intellect, as sensate and cognitive experiences merging into pictorial thought schemas.

A TRANSITION TO CRITICAL IMAGE

Probably the most efficient way of learning something significant about both the interior life and the patterned social behavior of individuals and families is to know something about the nature and scope of their images. Our images serve as our basic references for our ideas about the world. They are the bases for the characteristic behaviors we manifest in our relations with intimate others, and because our most important images have strong affective residuals associated with them, they are capable of involving wrathful indignation, brotherly love, or complete alienation, depending upon whether they are accepted or abused by those around us, whether they remain inaccessibly buried or disguised within us or are allowed expression such that our inner meanings and outer realities are compatible and bear a significant relationship to one another.

It is my contention that the hidden energy in the struggles that intimate partners manifest (and hence in the system developmental crises they generate) as they attempt to conceive, nurture, and perfect a family that "works" for the different individuals and for the whole system itself, is a special subset of images that I call *critical identity images*.

Features of the Critical Identity Image

An individual's critical identity images are distinguished from the larger family of sensory images by eight features:

1. They are primarily visual and spatial.
2. While their derivations are in past experience, they continue to influence present and future events to a significant degree,

and their formation does not stop in childhood or adolescence, but continues throughout life.

3. They are action sequenced, involving the self and at least one other significant person, who, together with the image-bearer, compose a scenario of action that is either implicit or explicit.

4. The psychopolitics (the behavior of an individual in relation to others) embedded in the originating image action are as important in later identity struggles as the content of the image, sometimes more important.

5. Through their specific *contents* (for example, the *routine humiliation* of a child by a parent while another *helplessly* looks on) and through the mood climates associated with these contents (for example, *gloom* or *heaviness*), critical identity images embody the thematic and qualitative character of the family system.

6. Within an individual's set of critical images, certain ones contain the instructions and formats for how the system's goals ought ideally to be defined (the model core purpose) and how the goals ought ideally to be realized (the homeostatic ideals). In other words, critical images contain the blueprints for model formation, and thus they define the scope of the system's development.

7. Critical identity images tend to have unusual vividness and intensity, what I call their *arousal value*. What people store in memory experience, then, is not only the special memory content of the image and the psychopolitical configuration, but an energy component associated with the original experience, reinforced by new experiences along the way.

8. Any new context similar in structure to the original identity image can invoke an emotional response and a behavioral response similar to what was experienced earlier. Therapists commonly try to neutralize the energies generated by these images and their collisions. Further they even attempt to get rid of the images. ("Look at it from her point of view . . ." etc.) I think both are mistaken strategies.

Whereas individuals may acquire many images, they tend to have but a handful of critical identity images. A clinical guess is that we acquire perhaps two or three key ones for each of the

major dimensions of our lives—some for our affect relations, some
for our power relations, and some for our spiritual-ideological
relations. Another guess is that we are especially open to the
formation of new critical identity images during the transition
periods that mark development throughout the individual lifecy-
cle.

During their identity struggles, people confront each other,
not with the competing critical identity images themselves (for
these are beneath the surface of awareness, and usually remain
there unless they spontaneously surface or are clinically elicited,
about which I shall say more later), but rather with *competing
claims* about reality: about how things *are* and how they *ought to
be*. Such claims are always specific and contextual. For example,
a man's failure to phone his wife as he promised may raise in his
wife a sense of abandonment in need. "For me, fidelity is unerring
reliability," she argues. "For me, fidelity is authenticity," her
husband counters.

These competing identity claims tend to be active assertions
of positive values. The *foundation image,* the memory picture
from which the positive identity claim is constructed, may be
either a positive or negative experience. Negative images of pain,
suffering and/or disappointment are transformed into positive
claims. Assertions intimate partners use in their ritual struggles
are based on positive representations of identity. Most people,
however, enter adult relationships with incomplete transformations. Their intimate relationships then become both context and
occasion for completion. Where this fails, the job may be passed
onto a therapist. Therapists who reach for the core image of pain
and suffering must not get stuck in their contemplation. The patient must move on to positive claims. Indeed, there are
therapists who, fascinated by suffering, assume that the patients
will eventually spontaneously abandon their pain. They would
realize their clinical aims better (and faster) were they to posi-
tively promote the transformation of negative to positive claims.

IN CONSIDERATION OF A CLINICAL THEORY

The developmental theory sketched out above is incorporated in the set of eight treatment procedures that I use to bring
about therapeutic change in couples (and families). This clinical

framework (in its beginning stages, just like the developmental theory on which it is based) has as its key feature the eliciting of critical identity images that are involved in maintaining the couple's ritual impasse.

Space does not allow an extensive account of these eight procedures. Instead, I will, after first setting down the clinical propositions that inform them, give an overview. This done, I shall focus on only one of these, eliciting the competing critical identity images, and discuss a therapy case.

Clinical Propositions

1. *If* what most clients bring to therapy is a system in crisis, that is, a system temporarily stalled in its normal developmental process;

    then the proper task of therapy work is to bring about a "successful" resolution of the crisis.
2. *If* a system crisis is an identity struggle taking place on four levels of system organization;

    then the effects of this crisis will be visible on all four levels, and, once the crisis is resolved through clinical intervention, the effects of this resolution should be visible on all four levels.
3. *If* these "levels" are, as proposed here, themselves systematically related;

    then changing the system's organization on any one level will effect changes on all other levels.
4. *If* the crisis, or identity struggle, begins at and is fueled by competing critical images;

    then a program of therapeutic change must directly or indirectly concern itself with defusing this image struggle, and, by helping the couple settle their competing identity claims, move the system beyond its developmental impasse and on its developmental course again, strengthened with a recent acquisition, a new or improved mechanism for reaching its goals.

Notice that again, first in the theoretical and now in the clinical domain, *image* is key. In life, as in therapy, images are the vehicles of identity, the currency of communication. Therapists are always dealing with images, with lost images, with twisted or distorted or painful images, and, in the least rewarding kind of therapy work, with a paucity of images. When dealing with two or more people in a conflict situation, systems therapists are inevitably dealing with competing images. Depending upon the therapists' theories, they may concern themselves directly with these images, or bypassing direct consideration of *meanings,* set out to repair and change the family's disabled structures by entering and altering the system on another level—the action level, for example, or the pattern level, or the model level.

Most systems therapists enter and alter the system on the pattern level of organization. What distinguishes one from another is *what they see* as "disabled" and how they describe these disabled structures. One systems therapist recommends that we focus on "sequences" that have disastrous, symptom-producing outcomes (Haley), another on "boundaries" that enmesh (Minuchin), another on faulty "communications" (Satir), and another on triangulations that prevent differentiation and growth (Bowen). Each of these important thinker-therapists recognizes disabled and disabling patterns, and each seeks to repair these patterns.

The therapist coming at system crisis from our developmental perspective will do so also. However, in viewing the family's problems as an unresolved developmental struggle most visibly characterized by a "breakdown in steering mechanisms" leading to a "ritual impasse" that is maintained by rigidly stereotyped (or "stuck") psychopolitical behavior configurations, this therapist will proceed in a way that is guided by the above clinical propositions. Specifically, he will organize his diagnostic and treatment efforts around locating the key ritual impasse, the representation of the system's key conflict pattern, and seek to free the system through an analysis of the identity struggle that is fueling the conflict, which necessarily includes changing the specific behaviors of individuals in the conflict pattern.

An Overview of the Treatment Process

EIGHT INTERDEPENDENT PROCEDURES

When a couple comes to therapy, its partners are in a developmental crisis. The first task of the therapist is to confirm that the problem(s) they present reveal the key ritual impasse.

Observing the ritual impasse, the therapist isolates the psychopolitical stances that have become frozen, and should do some preliminary work in altering these. Then, having the knowledge and power to promote change, the therapist awaits the propitious moment to elicit the critical images associated for each of the people with the impasse. When both partners have produced their images, the therapist expects and usually gets, some immediate progress and then a retrenchment, as the couple goes through a series of experiences of getting into the impasse and out of it again. The therapist uses this period to pin down more precisely the specific elements of each image, and then, in an effort to stabilize the couple's gains, he helps them to render visual their images, chiefly by helping each to develop a deepening understanding and appreciation of their own and the other's image. Next, the therapist directs the treatment such that each partner will shift that aspect of the psychopolitical stance that catalyzes the impasse behaviors in the other.

Although the treatment could easily end here, the two remaining optional steps, taken only by a renewed or renegotiated contract between clients and therapist, are important in this treatment approach. First, sharing the theory, the therapist encourages the couple to grasp the interlocking nature of the images and the inevitability of their mutual frustration, unless, of course, each partner is prepared to foreswear taking the crucial catalytic psychopolitical stance. Next, and finally, therapist and clients together generalize the knowledge thus far gained, exploring the applicability of theory to the couple's current, future, and past life experiences. This latter may entail helping the couple through concrete changes and decisions in the present, anticipating developmental issues that may arise in the future; and, through directly or indirectly working with the couple's families of origin and on the relation between their critical identity images, their recent conflicts, and their earlier family experiences, help differentiate past from the present and the future.

So, the eight procedures are:

1. locating the key ritual struggle;
2. isolating the psychopolitical configuration and making preliminary changes;
3. eliciting the competing critical identity images;
4. pinning down the image elements;

5. fixing the image, rendering it more visible, changing the meaning of the image;
6. changing the key (catalytic) psychopolitical moves;
7. sharing the theory with the couple; and
8. generalizing the theory and its applicability.

The Praegers

At this point, I will focus on one procedure: showing how I elicited the Praegers' identity images, and, incidentally, what came of that effort.

The Praegers, a childless couple married six years, came for therapy because their chronic anger and alienation made them wonder whether they should "stay married and have a child or chuck the whole thing." A physically handsome couple in their thirties, Janet and Robert had much going for them socially and professionally. Robert's aggressive intelligence and caring manners earned him a key managerial position with one of the fast rising nationally based real estate agencies, and Janet's career in "soft" research in the social sciences was, if tentative in these tight times, more secure than most midlevel freelance researchers.

In the initial mapping and problem-defining phase of the therapy, I established that the Praegers framed their difficulties in three life contexts: Robert's use of drugs to get high periodically ("Coke is the anodyne of the middle class in the '70s," he mocked.), a habit Janet opposed with violent disgust; Janet's troubled ambivalence about having a child (she even feared she was infertile), the decision around which Robert, though seemingly engaged, left mainly to his wife, which hindered more than helped, she objected; and finally, their sexual life, which they both agreed, was unsatisfactory, although not in shambles ("Robert is too available," Janet complained. "Janet is too evasive," Robert rejoined.).

My work with the Praegers was four months along before I was certain I had located the key ritual impasse, had isolated the psychopolitical stances that had become frozen in a disabling pattern, and had done some preliminary work altering these. As a result of this work, Robert became more authentically involved in the decision about having a child and Janet's angry sexual evasiveness was better understood, and became less pronounced once it was discussed in the light of a brief but inconsequential affair she had had. That is, some of the problems they faced in the relationship improved (as Robert shifted from a disabled *bystander* to an involved *follower* in the matter of having children, and Janet from a stuck *opposer* to a sometimes *mover* in matters sexual), but Robert and Janet's recurring struggle resurfaced periodically, seeming each time to temporarily nullify their gains, a situation that persisted until we did the image-work together. Obviously, I have not said all that goes into the steps one takes in locating the key impasse; however, here are four indicators I use as guidelines in deciding when to move ahead.

INDICATORS

1. *Identify the developmental task at which the couple is failing.* Though married six years and seriously committed to each other and to the marriage, the Praegers had failed to entirely solve one specific aspect of the first dilemma facing all couples: forming an attachment. Despite Janet's affair, commitment, loyalty, and fidelity were not problems. But, physical passion, or even more to the point, access to physical intimacy, was. They enjoyed their intimacy, physical and non-physical, when they could agree on how to get to it and what it should be like, but their preferred styles conflicted. Robert preferred *open system* routes (with strong expressions of personal need and interest, and consensual pathways to intimacy), while Janet preferred the ways of the *closed system* (with respect for privacy, differences in rhythms, and clear rules of approach and timing that both would scrupulously observe).

2. *Define the context of the identity struggle.* Three components define the "context" of a couples impasse, as I understand it: (1) the theme around which the struggle occurs and re-occurs; (2) the overall pattern or sequence of moves and the outcome of this sequence; (3) and the characteristic psychopolitical parts each partner plays in this pattern. *Availability,* and its complement *unavailability,* was the recurrent theme on which the Pragers' identity struggle fixed. Haplessly, the couple pursued parallel rather than joined routes to intimacy. Robert's ill-timed or too-strong moves catalyzed Janet's oppositional stances, which even in unconflictual contexts was quite characteristic for her.

3. *Client validity.* The clients themselves will usually place the main elements of their struggle in a specific domain and will pretty much agree when they have replayed that struggle in a therapy session. Thus, the therapist's diagnosis is firmed up through a natural test. "This is what happens," one partner

says after a disagreement or fight that ends in an impasse. "That's just the way it always happens," says the other.

4. *Therapist validity.* Whether or not the couple displays their impasse as clearly as I have just indicated, I usually delay concluding that I have confirmed the presence of the ritual impasse until I have witnessed essentially the same pattern at least two times.

The indicators provide a rather good idea of the-problem-in-context, which here means a theme around which a disabling pattern has been established and the parts each partner plays in maintaining that pattern. I have now glimpsed a breakdown of a steering mechanism and stuck psychopolitical stances around a theme that gets played out repeatedly in structurally similar life contexts.

ELICITING THE IMAGES

Robert and Janet showed up for their twelfth session in a terrible state, after a week of horror, disconnection, and despair. They had been to a party at which Janet's colleagues were informally feting a visiting academic dignitary, a renowned elder statesman. Robert had hit it off exceedingly well with the visitor despite their different ages and professional backgrounds. Together they held center stage a good part of the evening. Driving home, Robert, still full of himself, affectionately reached out for Janet's hand. It remained rigid, cold, unavailable. In the therapy session their merely dormant but still smoldering disagreement was rekindled once I moved to find out something about the context that had triggered it. Soon they were reliving their struggle, in which: Robert, from a position of self-assurance makes a strong bid, an affection-giving or affection-seeking move, without warning or preliminaries. Janet, put off by something in his manner, withholds, her anger gaining momentum as he defends his own moves and exaggerates her unavailability, at first accusingly and then in a manner "so pathetic" as to leave her no choice but to escalate her own defensive anger or remove herself. The rest of the week was hell.

This was the ritual impasse. The signs are unmistakable: righteous positioning; strong feelings, implacably defensive; escalation; painful pause; and finally, the hopeless shrug, structural evidence that love and greater wisdom are simply not available in the moment. Janet tried weakly to continue. Robert fell silent, a bit tearful. I stopped them, pursuing the image.

When a couple has spontaneously produced or heatedly re-produced *in the session* a recent crisis sequence that I believe to be *the* key ritual impasse, I attempt to elicit the competing critical identity images in the following way:

(Standing up and facing one image-bearer from a position behind the partner, I say: I would like you very quickly to survey all the events in your life that seem relevant to you right now. See if you can come up with a memory picture that is the basis for the position you are taking right now. *(Pause)* It may not be a single event that comes to mind, but it will be a picture or a scene that involves you and other key people in your life, a picture you have put together from important experiences and which is telling you how to be and how to behave right now. *(Some of this obviously is sheer filibuster, giving the clients time to conduct their interior image survey.)*

> *Robert's image:* I am a kid (about twelve). I am sick. *(At this time)* my parents are getting divorced. I am in bed. No one knows what I am suffering from *(a mysterious gastrointestinal disturbance for which he was hospitalized several times).* My father is at a distance, in the shadows or something. My mother is near me, but far from him. I want him to stay, so that they will stay together, but really for me. But he is looking away, distracted. I feel terribly sad. I have failed.

Once an image is produced, the therapist has two immediate, somewhat contradictory tasks: to recognize (or draw out if necessary) and respond to the feelings it has aroused (Robert cried deeply, then fell into a teary silence, drawing into himself); and to pin down enough of the concrete "elements" to "fix the picture" in awareness *(so that he can move on to the partner).* Between compassion and calculation, both tasks must get done, and more, the work with the partner. (The beginning therapist, engaged by his client's feelings, may linger too long, there; the experienced therapist, not long enough, what with the work yet to be done.) Done well, the therapist's next three clinical assignments (pinning down the image elements, rendering the images more visible, and changing the key catalytic psychopolitical moves) are made more efficiently manageable.

The experienced therapist balances emotional expression and concrete image details, for the goal of this therapy is, ultimately, not only the arousal of the strong effect associated with the image, but the restructuring of psychopolitical behavior predicated on the image and contained in it. So, the therapist, while permitting and encouraging the expression of feelings, also explores and enlarges on other structural details—visual, behavioral, conceptual—how old are you in this scene? in what room of the house does the scene take place? who else is there? what is mother wearing? how do you feel about what your brother is doing? who else is implicated in that part of the action, present or not present? "Fixing the image elements," then, is a preliminary shaping and setting down of the image's contextual, thematic, and action structure, a kind of holding action for the more thoroughgoing pinning down of the image elements that comes later. It is also a statement both to the image-bearer, as to what the therapist deems important, and, to the partner, that something new is going to happen.

Then the therapist moves on to the partner, standing now behind the spouse, and repeats the above instructions in a slightly abbreviated form. An important aside: I cannot be too insistent about the clinical importance of eliciting the two critical images in the same session, wherever possible. The contemporaneous exposure and subsequent complementary exploration of the competing images is largely responsible for the initial therapeutic gains that follow, gains that are concretely represented in a relaxation of the couple's struggle and a temporary resolution of the identity crisis. Such gains are based on a new readiness in each person to "let go" of the stuck psychopolitical maneuvers each is using in defense of their image and the reality it represents. A crucial factor in this therapy is the reciprocal validation of each person's reality claim, a process that begins with the contemporaneous exploration and mutual appreciation of the foundation images that underlie and precede these claims.

Janet's image: I am a little girl (between 6 and 8). *(When asked to "see" the memory picture, Janet, probably unaware of the gestural aspects of her overall communication, takes on what we later understand as her Shirley Temple pose— pursing her lips, tilting her head, letting her eyelids flutter in the sexy rhythm of the precocious child-woman pressed into the service of adult amusement.)* Daddy . . . my father has just come home from work or from one of his organizational meetings or something. Us kids *(Janet was the youngest of the girls and the third of four children)* are watching television. Daddy is sitting in his big chair *(now Janet frowns, her body stiffens—shoulders turned in and away from her audience—a gesture of defiance)* with his newspaper, his feet on a hassock, waiting for Mom to bring him his tea and crackers, on a tray no less. My brother and two sisters are at his feet. I know he wants me to say something cute and to sit on his lap. (He used to love my singing, and still does.) I like that but don't trust him. For years at about this time of my life he would make me perform for relatives or for his cronies. Does he really like me or is he just showing me off like one of his trophies *(awards from the many organizations he served, icons of identity he had all over our walls)?* I can't tell, really. But I decide to spoil it for him, usually. I make everybody work for my goodies. Especially you, Robert. ["You are worth it," he mutters.]

I would like to focus for a few moments on Janet's addendum to her image, and, because I think it will be most instructive, replay the process as if in slow motion, the better to follow its course.

But I decide to spoil it for him, Janet says, still "seeing" the memory image and her father in it, pausing then and saying, *usually.* Imagine the scenes passing at computer speed through her mind at this moment, the myriad times she sabotaged (that is, "opposed") her father's bidding (that is, refused to "follow" his "moves" to have her perform and entertain). I believe that Janet's pause here, and the generous, emphatically punctuated thought, *usually,* is a concession of great import—the very first stage in the development of a new move in her and the couple's psychopolitical repertoire, and the beginnings of change. As we continue our slow motion replay, we observe that at this moment Janet shifts her gaze downward, pulling forward from the image-revealing memory field that my image survey technique physically analogized in the area behind Robert.

I make everybody work for my goodies, she continues, with which the therapist, communicating approval directed to Janet, smiles broadly, his head arching upward and slowly down again, a gestural "YES!" Barely perceptibly, Janet smiles acknowledgment (a reward for the preliminary work the therapist had done on her characteristic psychopolitics): *Especially you, Robert.* Janet is a skilled researcher. At work, her style as a skeptical observer pays big dividends; in love, it contributes to disaster. Dropping the gestural quality of opposition in this particular communication is an immense breakthrough. In the vocabulary of psychopolitics, she has made a "pure move" toward Robert from the stance of an "uncontaminated bystander"; the choice is now Robert's—to go with the move or in some way to undermine it. Still half dazed from his brush with his own image, impressed by what Janet is doing with hers, Robert "follows:" *You are worth it,* he mutters.

Janet and Robert have joined in a breakthrough. On some level they now know that they have the means to transcend the ritual impasse, perhaps even to create together a new pattern out of their struggle.

But Janet and Robert will relapse. For retrenchment occurs fairly routinely following such breakthroughs. Almost on cue, the couple will appear at their next session having had "the best week together in years;" and then, in another week at their next meeting, they report that they are discouraged and reenact the ritual conflict pattern. I do not join them in despair. I see the retrenchment for what it is—a statement about the importance of their images and the meaning of those images. I use the retrenchment, then, as a remarkably rich source of additional information. I use, it, moreover, to stabilize and build on the kind of psychopolitical behavior changes witnessed in our slow motion replay. For such gains are the beginnings of structural change, and with their advent the hard work (image work, really) begins.

IMAGE WORK

Reduced to essentials, the goals of (systems) therapy are really quite simple. They are to bring about, first, a change in *stuck psychopolitical behaviors* and, second, a change in the *meaning of an identity image*. Simple to state, but not always easy to do, as we all know.

In the Praegers' ritual impasse, Robert is a stuck mover and Janet a stuck opposer. From my analysis of the Praegers' psychopolitical behavior configuration in the system mapping (or diagnostic) phase of the treatment, I learned that in contexts where physical intimacy was the goal, Robert had to learn how to *bystand* (e.g., gauge Janet's readiness and pacing requirements in sex and intimacy before initiating) and *follow* (e.g., wait for Janet to initiate intimacy moves some of the time); and that Janet had to learn how to *move* (e.g., initiate when she was interested and/or indicate what she *was* interested in when intimacy was *not* her goal) and *follow* Robert's move some of the time without opposing.

In setting out to change the couple's behaviors, it is important for the therapist to track the relationship between each partner's psychopolitics in the impasse, in the positive identity claim and in the foundation image.

In Robert's foundation image, he is literally and figuratively a disabled mover, a boy who gets sick in order to draw his father back into the family. In pinning down the elements of his image, we learned also that Robert was either a too cautious or an easily injured bystander, that his father was an irrepressible mover who insisted upon directing his affections outside whatever system he was in, and that Robert's mother was an altogether disabled follower; these related behaviors being typical in family contexts in which the seeking of affection and intimate contacts were at issue. In the transformation of his foundation image into a positive identity claim, Robert developed as an attractive, assertive man fully expecting to be recognized by women and men alike; and, despite periodic lapses with Janet and quite frequent lapses with his father, Robert succeeded in many of his social contexts in having his claims realized.

In Janet's foundation image, she is the prototypical stuck opposer. From this stance, we learn in our pinning down of the image elements, that she feels disdain for her siblings, who she sees as grovelling insipidly for attention. As the family's generous "supplier," her mother's psychopolitical and imagistic character is formed primarily around serving others—the prototypical follower. Mother and siblings, therefore, infuse the father's self-proclaimed, presumptuous self-worth with even greater value. In the transformation of *her* image into a positive identity claim, Janet retains the opposition stance of her foundation image as a central feature of her style, and makes it work for her. (Later, in its course, when the therapy has succeeded in adding *following* to her repertoire, in contexts where previously it was missing, Janet "claimed:" *I grant the necessity of these new ways of acting, David, but I am at core an opposer. It will always be that way some of the time because I like it that way.*) In her current, as in previous, employments, for example, she was routinely rewarded for her incisive critical judgments, and she was appreciated by friends for her impeccable integrity and strong views. All in all, she had developed a successful style, though the nature of her style led inevitably to more clashes and impasses with intimates than Robert's did outside the relationship.

Within this relationship, Janet's and Robert's preferred psychopolitics clash horrendously, especially when they are asserting their identity claims in affectional contexts. Expecting, nay needing to be rewarded for his direct offerings of affections, as well as responded to when bidding for affections, the puzzled Robert becomes more and more confused as the impasse escalates, before dissolving altogether in hurtful retreat. Expecting and needing to be allowed her skeptical caution before committing herself to an intimate course of action, Janet intensifies her opposition mercilessly in the escalating impasse before turning away in disgust from her now weakened suitor.

Once these relationships—between the couple's behavior in the ritual impasse, in the positive identity claims, and in their foundation images—are established, a design for the remaining therapeutic program is a relatively simple matter. Implementing it depends on the therapist's style and technical mastery and the idiosyncracies of the case, especially the progress each person has made in transforming original foundation images into workable and efficient identity claims in close relationships. While the details are beyond the scope of this chapter, the following observations on economy and techniques are relevant.

Economy. All therapies must question their economics. Like all therapies, this one strives for an economy of means in the midst of implacable complexity. If therapists agree to take on the kind of image-work I am describing here, they must deal with compelling tendencies to drift away from the key structures contained in the impasse. Call it resistance—the couple will distract you with their complexity, finding new contexts for replaying the same stuck psychopolitics. Striving for economy of means, therefore, means striving for structural clarity and holding the line, or at least knowing where and when to draw the line. At its simplest, this requires no more than being responsible for deliberate selective attention. It means bringing the clients back into focus when they drift or present new crises or slip into yet another retrenchment around an old crisis. Whatever the case, a firm refocusing on the image and its structures is essential (assuming, of course, you are pretty sure that your original diagnosis of the key ritual is on target and is not subject to review). As you succeed in resisting their induction, insisting instead on structural clarity, the clients will be grateful.

Techniques. Family therapy has discovered some useful techniques for changing structures (e.g., the artful use of tasks and paradoxical interventions). But where the therapist's goals are even moderately ambitious, as they often are and must be, techniques, as such, eventually lose their power. I have little faith in a philosophy of change oriented too much in utility. The family therapy community opens itself to the criticism of false claims when it fosters the illusion that it is capable of unlimited efficacy. Technology *is* limited; the more so in complex human affairs. Easy access to change through programmed techniques cannot take the place of thought, discovery, and hard work. The goals of "changing key psychopolitical behaviors and the meaning of an image" are moderately ambitious goals. In pursuing these goals, therapists are free to draw upon many techniques, from their favorite sources and from the resources of their own invention. The method I am describing is not dependent upon specific techniques, not even the image-survey technique, that as I have noted, I often use in eliciting the couple's images. This and other techniques (role play, paradoxical maneuverings, video playback, tasks, rendering the image metaphorically on canvas, sculpture, slide projection blow-ups of the images, and rational persuasion) were my choices.

CHANGING THE MEANING OF AN IMAGE

On this subject, I am inclined to be dogmatic: We do not change images. We change behaviors associated with an image, and we change the *meaning* of an image. Thus, I must enlarge the second goal of therapy to mean *bringing about a change in the meaning of an image without disturbing the image itself*. The issue is as much technical as it is philosophical, though it has equal shades of both. However, only the former interests us here—i.e., even if you thought it *good* to change another's image you could not; for these memory imprints are indelible, they do not erase—a therapy that tries to alter them will be uneconomical.

In this systems therapy, the goals of changing the meaning of an image and changing the key psychopolitical behaviors associated with that image are interactive. In other systems therapy they are not. In "staging" changes, I will usually put the greater emphasis on first changing behaviors, since meanings change more slowly and take a greater therapeutic effort and more time. Still, a very sound way to change meaning is via a change in behavior—thus my great concern with preliminary psychopolitical behavior change. The best way to look at it is as a feedback loop, where success in the one realm leads to success in the second, which makes greater success possible in the first.

In doing image-work, remember that an image is usually not produced whole. The details of feeling, attitudes, setting, and behavior, and the relationship between and among thematic and behavioral elements of image structure, are solicited through the ongoing therapeutic dialogue. Pinning the Praegers' image elements down took place over a period of about four to six meetings following their original surfacing. Fixing the image took place over another three to five meetings. Work with other couples indicates that these are fairly typical. A pragmatic rule is that the images are not fixed until the couple understands fully how their images have been interacting in and maintaining the ritual struggle; and moreover, the couple can confidently abort and avoid new struggles with the help of an expanded psychopolitical repertoire. The procedure of pinning down the image elements may take weeks. Gradually, however, the image elements come together to form a coherent articulation of how past and present collide and coalesce, an articulation that is literally thematic as well as symbolic, with each element adding a dimension to a central thematic core. Each partner's separate themes come together in a single thematic context that has both disparate and complementary elements. For example, Robert's fear of *abandonment is need* and Janet's intractable *rejection of presumptive power* result in sexual impoverishment and despair in which meanings having to do with quest and demand, caution and rejection, distraction and unavailability are distorted and confused. Such distortions of intentional meaning, defensively maintained by psychopolitical rigidities are the targets of the therapist's image work.

Recently, I have been experimenting with a new technique for helping to fix the image. I literally render the images more visible by setting them down on canvas. Here, the therapist and an artist collaborate. In two meetings with the couple, the artist explores the concrete details of each image in turn and, with the therapist's and the couple's help, metaphorically transforms the images. The resulting painted image achieves a dramatic enlargement of meaning, and an economy and beauty of its own. As a clinical technique its aim is to help in changing the meaning of the couple's images. It does this by deploying its contents toward creative ends; by sharing the power of personal disclosures with the partner, who now is a sympathetic expert on its subject;

through the power of distanced perspective, in which the importance of the "visible" part of the "rendering the image more visible" is vital. But remember: truth is not in the mechanization of technique.

My technique seems to help, even to work, but I do not feel wed to it, and in fact, I use it sparingly. With another couple I might use sculpture or no such dramatic technique at all. But whatever techniques I choose, I will be seeking to help the couple to extend the possibilities inherent in their own images and in the partner's.

It should now be evident that, in conducting the image work (eliciting the images, pinning down their elements, and fixing the images), the therapist's aims are to provide an opportunity for a sympathetic exploration of the quintessential themes and characteristic behaviors in each partner's identity images; to raise into consciousness an understanding of the ramifications each one's themes and behaviors have on the other; to encourage a reappraisal of one's own negative foundation experiences, so that the destructive or painful elements can be seen as bases for positive identity transformations; and to assist each partner in developing a sympathetic appreciation of the other's image elements.

Such changes in the meanings of the Praegers' images first began when I managed to unglue some of the psychopolitical rigidities that were supporting their impasse. Change continued when the contemporaneous disclosure of the two foundation images (both negative in sign in this instance) allowed Janet and Robert to share a compassionate recognition of the painful origins of the very reality assertions that seemed so threatening.

Change in each person's perceptions got its next big impetus from a series of interventions carefully designed to modify those particular unproductive elements of style that had been identified as *the* key catalytic behaviors responsible for maintaining the impasse. Another boost toward change came with my publicized refusal to be distracted by the seductive complexities they insisted on bringing in for consideration. (I must confess that I was not always perfect in resisting the temptations to sacrifice what I have called *structural clarity* for my counterproductive voyeurism. But the practical lesson of this mistake has served me well with other couples who followed the Praegers.)

With each succeeding examination of the tedious reapplication of the same old strategies of style and distortions of intentional meaning in new contexts, the Praegers began to assimilate the changes in perception, that by now were well underway. Each now knew that the other's identity claim was valid in its own right and that the other's reality wasn't crazy at all, or life threatening. Having been shown by example how their painful images could become an extraordinarily clear mirror of the truth of their lives, they could appreciate the poetry of their pain for the first time. Thus, as each one found their private world confirmed and enlarged, a change in the meaning of their image took place. No longer seeking to alter the other's perceptions, their perceptions of the other's premises were altered. A second change in the meaning of an image had taken place.

With the realizing of both goals of therapy, the Praegers resolved an identity crisis of long duration. In about four or five additional meetings, I covered the seventh and eighth procedures—sharing the theory with the couple and generalizing its application. In the course of the latter, Robert and Janet focused on their relationships with their fathers, both of whom played key parts in the couple's life, as they had in the critical images.

The Praegers appear now to be back on developmental course again, strengthened with vastly more successful strategies for realizing their goals, especially, but not exclusively, the goals of intimacy. In the period of eight months following my therapeutic contact with them, they have continued to solidify the positive changes already realized and to make additional ones—a residential shift that allows for much greater neighborhood involvement, for example, and changes in style of living and playing that leave much more time both for solitary intimate engagement and for expanded friendships. Not unexpectedly, the decision to have a child has been tabled for the time being; for with a successful facing of some of the dilemmas of attachment, they are able to make clearer distinctions between developmental tasks. Accordingly, they have all but consciously decided to enjoy the rewards of attachment for a time longer, and to focus next on issues of industry and affiliation before taking on the issues of inclusion. From being privy to the two critical images I have shared in this presentation and others not shared (or addressed with them), it would not surprise me if Robert and Janet find themselves in the future in another normal developmental impasse.

REFERENCES

Kantor, D. & Lehr, W. Inside the family: Toward a theory of family process. San Francisco, Jossey-Bass, 1975.

Index